Tableau Desktop

A Practical Guide for Business Users

Jane A. Crofts

Copyright © 2015 Jane A. Crofts

All rights reserved.

FOREWORD

Tableau Software's mission is to help people see and understand their data. Their belief that anyone that has data will benefit from being able to visualize it, analyze it and take actions underpins everything that they do.

Tableau Desktop enables the people that own the data ask questions of that data. To play with the data and create visualizations that enable them to find answers quicker than ever before.

Tableau removes the need to rely on a reporting service, using a simple drag and drop interface, industry good practice, anyone can analyze data. Every business has data, but if you cannot analyze it and get value from it, then it is worthless.

No longer do people have to spend hours on spreadsheets trying to find that one bit of information. Tableau shows you the answer, faster and easier so that you can spend your time doing more important things, like running your business.

Matt Francis, Tableau Zen Master

FROM THE AUTHOR

I was introduced to Tableau by my uncle, Hugh. "Janey," he said, "This is *<feel free to insert the name of any cutting-edge data analysis software package>* on drugs". Within hours, I too was hooked. Tableau just made sense. It was easy. It was beautiful. It was fast. It was fantastic. Tableau had its new biggest fan!

Since that auspicious day, I have done nothing but Tableau. I now lead a niche consulting firm specializing in all things Tableau. We don't do anything else. As an Alliance Partner of Tableau Software, and one of the first Partners in Australia, we have worked with organizations of all sizes, across all industries, in both public and private sectors to help share the Tableau-love.

From creating amazing business intelligence suites — powered by Tableau, of course — to mentoring teams of analysts in their use of Tableau, I've had the opportunity to lead and be part of many Tableau adoptions. The stories and experiences from these client engagements are now presented for you in this book, a practical guide to Tableau Desktop, written specifically for business users.

This book has been designed to take beginner and intermediate Tableau Desktop users through the key functions and features they most likely need, and therefore use, when working with Tableau Desktop in their business.

This is a collection of my top tips for quickly getting traction with Tableau Desktop. This book provides a step-by-step process for quickly connecting to a range of data sources; building useful calculations; creating charts, tables and other visualizations to unleash the insights that Tableau is famous for and then sharing these findings with others.

Jane A Crofts

CONTENTS

Getting Started **15**

1. Introducing the Tableau suite of products 15
2. Which version should I be using? 15
3. Gaining traction with Tableau in your business 17
4. A quick overview of key features and phrases 18

It's time to change the way you think about data **25**

1. Clarify your questions 26
2. Catalogue your data sources 27
3. Correct your data 28
4. Chart your data 28
5. Communicate your findings 29

From Data to Done: four phases of Tableau fun! **30**

Data **31**

1. Choosing the right data connector 31
2. Connecting to data 37
   - *Worked example: Connecting to data* *39*
   - *Worked example: "Drag and Drop" data connections* *47*
   - *Worked example: Copy and paste data directly into Tableau Desktop* ... *50*
3. Formatting data 52
   - *Worked example: Changing default number formats* *54*
   - *Worked example: Changing default number format to currency* *61*
   - *Worked example: Changing default date formats* *68*

4. Blending data 72
   - *Worked example: Basic data blending* 73
   - *Worked example: Not-so-basic data blending* 75
   - *Worked example: Detailed data blending / custom relationships* 77
   - *Worked example: Blending sample data sets* 81
5. Field Names and Aliases 92
   - *Worked example: Identifying and changing aliases* 95
6. Calculated Fields 98
   - *Worked example: Creating calculated fields* 103
7. Saving and sharing data sources 107
   - *Worked example: Publishing to Server* 108
   - *Worked example: Share data sources on shared drives* 113
8. Editing and replacing data sources 114
   - *Worked example: Editing existing data sources* 115
   - *Worked example: Replacing existing data sources* 118
   - *Worked example: Working with metadata* 121
9. Using extracts 121
   - *Worked example: Creating an extract* 123
   - *Worked example: Automatically refreshing extracts* 126

Details 132

1. Bar & Line Charts 132
   - *Worked example: Creating bar charts* 133
   - *Worked example: Creating line charts* 144
2. Geographic Maps 157
   - *Worked example: Creating geographic maps* 158
3. Scatter Plots 169
   - *Worked example: Creating scatter plots* 170

4.	Pie Charts	177
	Worked example: Creating pie charts	*178*
5.	Dual Axis Charts	188
	Worked example: Creating dual axis charts	*189*
6.	Crosstabs and tables	210
	Worked example: Creating crosstabs or tables	*211*
7.	Using Filters and Actions	218
	Worked example: Using filters	*219*

Dashboards 232

1.	Building wow-worthy dashboards	232
2.	Basic dashboard components	233
	Worked example: Creating a basic dashboard	*234*
	Worked example: Formatting dashboards	*238*
3.	Headline measures	242
4.	Filter across multiple items	243
	Worked example: Filtering across multiple items	*244*
5.	Interactivity	253
6.	Floating vs tiles	256

Done (time to share!) 259

1.	Tableau Server	259
2.	Tableau Online (Tableau Server 'in the cloud')	260
3.	Tableau Public	261
4.	Tableau Reader	263
5.	Print to PDF	264

The Finishing Touch 265

1. Removing lines / grid lines / outlines 265
   Worked example: Removing lines, gridlines and outlines 266
2. Copy / paste formatting 272
   Worked example: Copy and paste formatting 273
3. Custom color palettes 276
   Worked example: Creating custom color palettes 277
4. Custom shapes 280
   Worked example: Creating custom shape palettes 281

Where to from here? 283

Index 287

JANE A. CROFTS

GETTING STARTED

1. INTRODUCING THE TABLEAU SUITE OF PRODUCTS

The Tableau suite of products includes Tableau Desktop, Tableau Server, Tableau Online and Tableau Public. This book is focused on Tableau Desktop; however, it does touch on Tableau Server, Tableau Online and Tableau Public and discusses the ways you can use each of them to share the dashboards and visualizations you have developed in Tableau Desktop.

2. WHICH VERSION SHOULD I BE USING?

A lot of clients I worked with would often get caught out when choosing (or rather, after they have chosen) the version of Tableau Desktop that they will be using to build the visualizations. If people ask me which version they should use — I immediately ask them, "What version of Tableau Server are you going to be publishing on?"

More often than not, Tableau Server is installed and configured by the IT department as part of an overall enterprise architecture which comes with its own governance, procedures and processes — i.e.: this is a lot harder for IT to change than it is for a business user to download and access an earlier version of Tableau Desktop.

Why is it important to consider which version you should be using? Because you cannot "publish down". That is, if you have developed a visualization in Tableau Desktop 9.0 and your organization is running Tableau Server 8.3, you are not going to be able to publish your 9.0 visualization to the 8.3 server environment. Essentially you want to be running the same version of desktop as the version of Server that has been rolled out. You can, however, "publish up", meaning if you have a workbook from 8.3, you can publish it to a 9.0 version of Tableau Server.

So — the real question is, "What version server is my organization hosting"? It is very important that if there is an enterprise installation of Tableau Server that you and any other analysts within the business work with a compatible version of Tableau Desktop. If your Tableau Server is 8.3, make sure you're using Tableau Desktop 8.3 or earlier. If your Tableau Server is 9.0, make sure you're using anything up to and including 9.0, etc.

If you are familiar with products such as Microsoft Word and Microsoft Excel, you will know that you are able to effectively "save down" to other versions — i.e. you can create a document in the latest version Microsoft Word but "save it down" to an earlier version to share with colleagues who may not have the latest installation. This backwards compatibility is not possible in Tableau Desktop. This is important to keep in mind particularly when you are looking to share your workbooks with others.

Unfortunately this is quite a common problem and one that I've had to work through with many clients to date. Because the latest versions of Tableau are always so easy to access — it's no surprise that when people get excited about Tableau they immediately look to install the latest version and get started right away!

Too often I've seen cases where a business user has developed some pretty cool dashboards and wants to publish them to the server, only to find they are using a more recent version of Tableau Desktop than their organization's deployment of Tableau Server. This leaves us with an amazing viz that can't be published and a disappointed (and frustrated!) Tableau Desktop user. The only thing to do in this case is to either rebuild the viz from scratch in a compatible version of Tableau Desktop or copy individual worksheets and dashboards into a compatible version of Tableau Desktop and then publish the new workbook to the server.

This book does not tie itself to a specific version of Tableau Desktop. This book is designed to be used across multiple versions of Tableau Desktop, as it focuses more on the business processes and use of the software as opposed to the specific skills and features that are inherent in different versions. For more details regarding the specific versions, visit www.tableau.com.

3. GAINING TRACTION WITH TABLEAU IN YOUR BUSINESS

As with the introduction of any new software to a business, it can be a bit of an uphill challenge to shifting end-user behavior and getting your users to actually use the software! I have found the fastest and simplest way to improve uptake of Tableau across any business is to start showing results in Tableau.

Make the most of any opportunity you get to show off your interactive visualization or dashboards, either on your desktop screen or laptop, or up in lights on a meeting room projector or big screen. Your Tableau wizardry will very quickly begin to be noticed. Sharing packaged workbooks (and a link to Tableau Reader) alongside other reports that are emailed out will give users the option to see the product for themselves.

You will most likely find a couple of "early adopters" throughout the business who will get very excited at the speed, the beauty and the simplicity of your Tableau vizes. Once these "early adopters" see and use your intuitive, interactive and insightful dashboards and visualizations, they will start wanting more and more... increasing demand across the business for this type of work. Then, BAM! Tableau is now just part of the way you too do business.

4. A QUICK OVERVIEW OF KEY FEATURES AND PHRASES

Before we go much further, it is a pertinent time to point out some of the lingo or terminology that will be used throughout this book. Tableau has some unique terms and also uses terms in different ways than we may be used to. Knowing these terms — and how they are used — helps to describe the way we use Tableau Desktop.

All of the terms and terminology that are important to know are also provided in index at the back of this book. However, here are a few points that you should know from the beginning that will help with your understanding of this book as you progress through it.

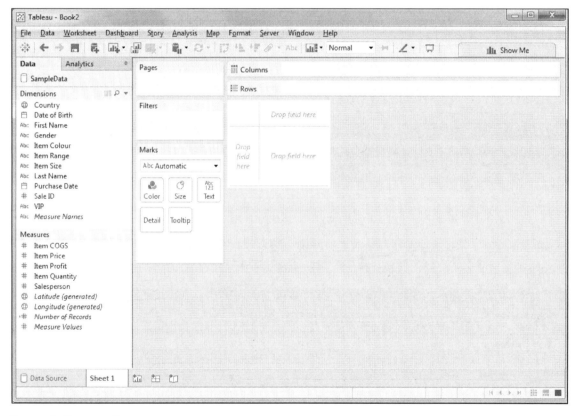

FIGURE 1: TABLEAU DESKTOP

Data Source

FIGURE 2: DATA SOURCE

A data source is like a template or a connection to a data source which you have customized with various calculated fields, metadata or formatting you have added. I like to think of a data source as a data template. When we create data sources, we are not editing the data — we are editing the picture-frame through which we will view of the data.

For example, if I have a numerical field that I know contains currency data: I can format that field in my data source to represent itself as Australian Dollars with two decimal places so that every time I use my data source I will see values displayed in Australian Dollars. However, the underlying data at the data original source will always stay untouched. We are editing the shape and display formats of the data; we are not touching the underlying data.

Dimensions and Measures

Tableau automatically generates a list of dimensions and measures from the data sources you have created:

Dimensions

Dimensions are the fields that we use to categorize data, to describe and to define data.

Measures

Measures are values that we want to perform a function on; for example we may want to count a value or we may want to apply a mathematical formula to a value.

You can have numbers that are dimensions. For example, you may have a key or an index to a particular category of data. This would mean that we would have a numerical field in the dimensions as opposed to in the measures.

In the event that Tableau has categorized the dimensions and measures incorrectly when a data source is created, you are able to simply drag and drop the measure from the measures field and drag it into the dimensions pane — doing that will allow you to use that field as a dimension as opposed to a measure.

FIGURE 3: DIMENSIONS AND MEASURES

You can also do the same for when a field appears in a dimension. For example, if there a number that Tableau has recognized as a number and interpreted to be an index or unique identifier, but it is actually a value you want to perform a function on (such as a sale price you might want to add up over time), you can drag that from dimensions to measures and use it in that way.

Cards

Cards are the way we refer to the boxes or areas of the Tableau Desktop environment. The number of cards that we have depends on what we have chosen to display as a base minimum; however, you will always see cards for pages, filters and marks.

Filters card

The filters card is where we can control the filtering in and out of different variables that we have drawn across from the dimensions and measures.

Marks card

The marks card is perhaps the most important card when we are trying to edit and format the display of our visualization.

FIGURE 4: FILTERS AND MARKS CARDS

Shelves

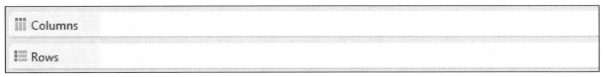

FIGURE 5: COLUMN AND ROW SHELVES

In addition to cards, we also refer to shelves — there is a column shelf and row shelf. Dragging dimensions or measures onto shelves creates columns and rows in the visualization. These will be discussed in more detail in later sections of the book.

Pills

Throughout this book, you will see many references and instructions to drag pills onto various cards and shelves. Pills refer to the visual representation of a field when it is being dragged or placed onto a card or shelf.

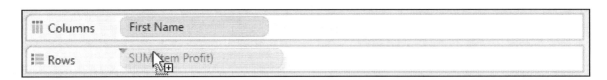

FIGURE 6: DRAGGING PILLS TO SHELVES

You will notice that when a field is being dragged or placed on a card or shelf, it appears inside a blue or a green container with rounded edges that look like a pill or tablet. Where you see references to 'dragging a pill to the column shelf', it simply means dragging a field from the dimensions or measures to sit inside the column shelf.

FIGURE 7: PILLS ON SHELVES

Viz and Vizes

Another key term that you will see used throughout this book is viz or vizes. The term viz or vizes applies to the visualization we have created. A viz can be one component of a dashboard or a standalone chart or viz can also be used to reference an entire dashboard.

Worksheets and Dashboards

In Tableau Desktop, we create dashboards for ourselves and for our users to interact with. These dashboards are comprised of multiple worksheets. The way we create a dashboard is to build individual worksheets that contain individual pieces of our dashboard and then bring them together.

Worksheets

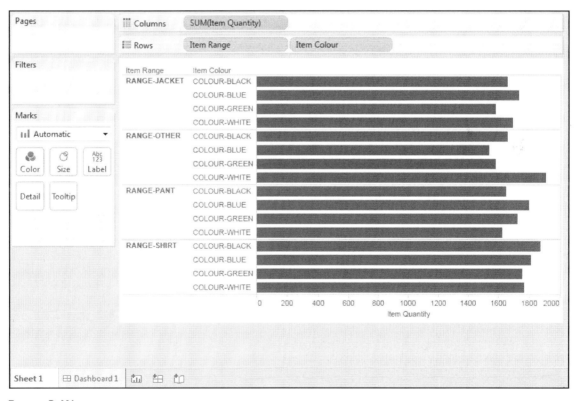

FIGURE 8: WORKSHEETS

Dashboards

We can then create our dashboard or viz with enhancements such as interactions, filtering, etc.

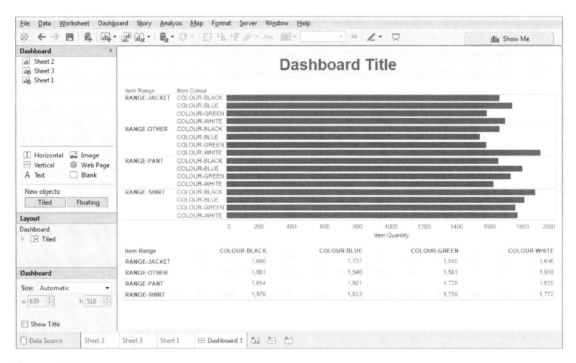

FIGURE 9: DASHBOARDS

IT'S TIME TO CHANGE THE WAY YOU THINK ABOUT DATA

One of the more common frustrations I see when I work with clients is that the data "doesn't work" or isn't behaving the way they expected it to. More often than not, analysts and business users have become accustomed to the way they are receiving data from their enterprise systems — be they cubes, tables, text files and so on — and have tailored the way they use data based on those formats. Business users tend to think "get the data first, then we'll see what we can find in it".

> *"It's time to change the way we think about data."*

Instead of a "data first" mentality, I believe we should be asking "What is it I'm trying to analyze / investigate / solve?" By switching to a "problem first, data second" approach, we free our analyses from the constraints of existing data sets and structures, opening our analyses up to a new way of thinking. Instead of asking, "What can I do with this data?" we can ask, "How is my business performing?" and "Why is performance declining / stagnant / improving?" We move from "what" to "why".

To support this change in thinking, I have developed the following framework to act as a set of prompts whenever a new project or problem presents itself:

Step 1:   **Clarify** your questions

Step 2:   **Catalogue** your data sources

Step 3:   **Correct** your data

Step 4:   **Chart** your data

Step 5:   **Communicate** your findings

1. CLARIFY YOUR QUESTIONS

You have to clarify the questions that the business needs answered. Think about your organizational Key Performance Indicators (KPIs) — what are your company's measures of success? Turn these into questions.

If a KPI is to improve performance of "X Service", then what questions could we ask to measure performance? What questions could we use to understand the factors contributing to that performance and identify areas for improvement or areas of success to be replicated across the business?

These are the real questions that need to be answered and once we have clarified these questions, it is time to think about how we're going to answer them. If business problems and questions are clearly defined, this will make identifying the data required (and therefore the data sources required) a lot easier.

2. CATALOGUE YOUR DATA SOURCES

With a clear set of questions, the task of defining and then sourcing data becomes a lot easier. I would encourage everyone at this stage to stop, think and then think again. Think past the data sets that you know already exist and think about the range of systems and processes in your business that generate and collect data.

Does your Human Resources system capture data that could be used in conjunction with data from your Sales system to identify key characteristics of sales people who outperform others?

Does your Accounting system capture data that could be blended with your customer data to identify trends in activity based on geographic locations?

If you are part of a team or department of analysts, I strongly recommend taking the time — as a group — to collectively think through your key enterprise systems and data sets and invest some time in preparing a suite or range of data sources which bring together the extensive content and data knowledge of the team. These new and expanded combinations of data sources will allow for some fascinating analysis and exploration later on!

3. CORRECT YOUR DATA

A key step in working with Tableau Desktop is the creation of data sources. This process is discussed in detail throughout this book, however, it is worth noting here that this step will take some time. The majority of clients I work with underestimate the amount of time this step will take. Yes, Tableau has some fantastic features and functions to make this step easier, but there are still a number of things we need to do to prepare our data to make our analysis and exploration in Tableau Desktop as smooth as possible.

However, most data preparation tasks are largely a "once off" activity that can be reused by different Tableau worksheets and dashboards if done properly. These data sources can then be shared across the team, indeed the entire business, allowing fast connection to well-prepared data to support meaningful analysis.

As more and more data sources are created and shared, working with Tableau Desktop becomes much faster and smoother, data blending opportunities become greater, and the analysts' role shifts from "data dude" to "insight guru".

4. CHART YOUR DATA

This step refers loosely to any visualization and dashboard. Make sure you're telling the right story with your presentation. The tools and features in Tableau Desktop that will assist you with this step are described in detail throughout this book.

5. COMMUNICATE YOUR FINDINGS

The driving force, indeed the clearly articulated mission of Tableau Software, is **to help people see and understand data**. To me, the best part of creating vizes and dashboards with Tableau Desktop is sharing these with your stakeholders.

Maybe your data visualization has identified a new product opportunity? Maybe your analysis and forecasting has predicted a pending downturn in sales that needs to be countered with an innovative marketing strategy? Perhaps your interactive monitoring systems have freed up resources across the business that can now be deployed to solving new business problems? Whatever you've created, designed or discovered, I guarantee it is going to be met with at least one "wow".

So share your work as widely and as often as your business rules allow: publish interactive vizes of your annual report on your company website, run dedicated monitors across your office to show performance against targets, replace traditional management and board reporting with interactive dashboards accessed on iPads and Android tablets. However you decide to share your findings, make sure you listen out for the squeals of delight that come from your recipients!

FROM DATA TO DONE: FOUR PHASES OF TABLEAU FUN!

Working with Tableau Desktop really comes down to four key phases:

1. Data
2. Details
3. Dashboards
4. Done

You may have noticed that the first stage, data, is the longest section of this book. In my experience, I have found that many people underestimate the importance of getting the data phase right from the beginning. The good news is, for every minute of investment you make in this phase, you will be rewarded tenfold in the ease and results of future phases!

DATA

1. CHOOSING THE RIGHT DATA CONNECTOR

Tableau provides a range of native connectors with built in processes to make connecting to a wide range of data sources as simple as possible. These native connectors are continually being built upon, so if your enterprise data warehouse or business intelligence platform isn't represented in the existing list, chances are it's already on Tableau's product roadmap for future releases!

If we have an Excel file or a text file, such as a comma separated value (.csv) file, there are native connectors that will guide you through the data connection process. Similarly, if we want to connect to a data source that exists on a server, such as a Microsoft SQL Server installation or any other enterprise data warehouse, there are native connectors which will guide you through each step of the data connection process.

To view the current range of native connectors, you can click on "Connect to Data" as shown in Figure 10: Connect to Data - Option 1.

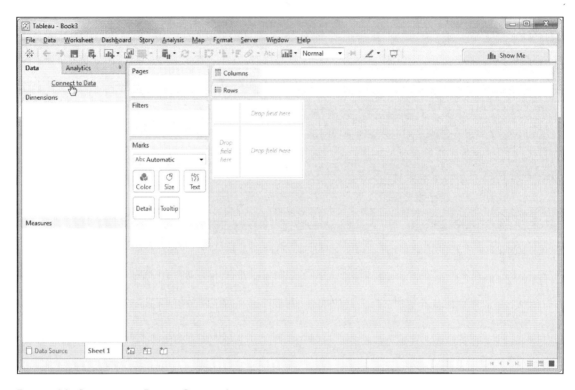

FIGURE 10: CONNECT TO DATA - OPTION 1

Alternatively, you can also select Data from the toolbar and click 'New Data Source', as shown in Figure 11: Connect to Data - Option 2.

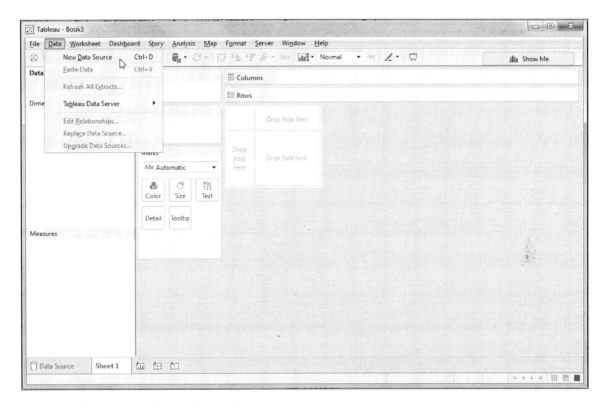

FIGURE 11: CONNECT TO DATA - OPTION 2

The available connection types are then listed as shown in Figure 12: Connect to Data - Connection Types (for v9.0 and beyond) or Figure 13: Connect to Data - Connection Types (earlier releases).

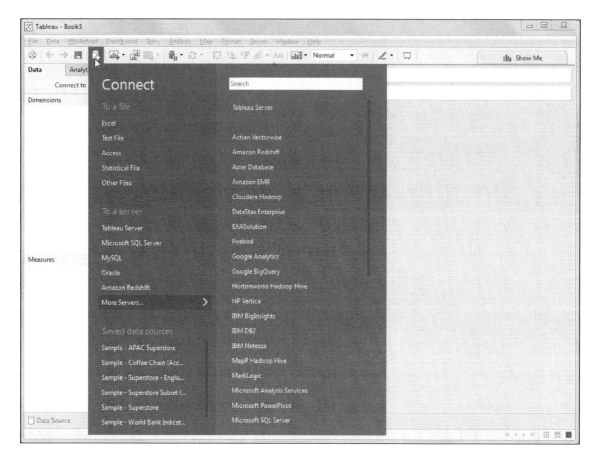

FIGURE 12: CONNECT TO DATA - CONNECTION TYPES

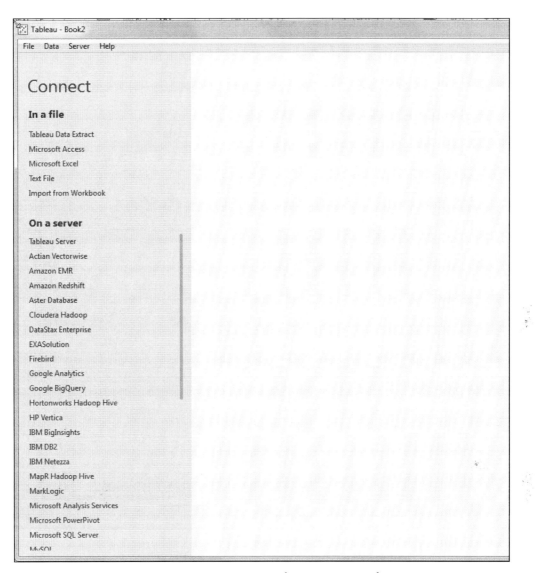

FIGURE 13: CONNECT TO DATA - CONNECTION TYPES (EARLIER RELEASES)

Finally, when you first open Tableau Desktop, the welcome screen also lists available connection types on the left of the screen as shown in Figure 14: Connect to Data - Connection Types from Welcome Screen.

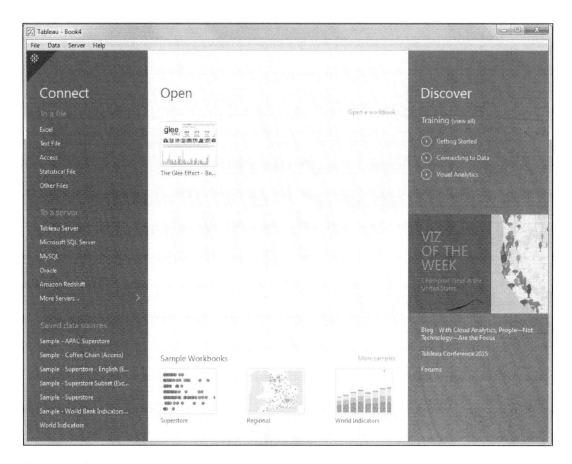

FIGURE 14: CONNECT TO DATA - CONNECTION TYPES FROM WELCOME SCREEN

2. CONNECTING TO DATA

When you open Tableau Desktop, you will either be presented with the home screen which contains thumbnails of your recent workbooks, an option to connect to various data sources and an option to "discover", which includes samples of data sources and business created by Tableau and also Viz of the Week.

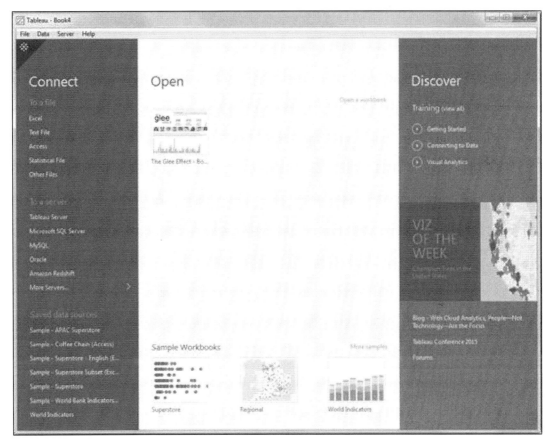

FIGURE 15: WELCOME SCREEN

In older versions of Tableau, you will certainly see the "Connect and Open" sections, but you will not see the "Discover" section as it is new to version 9.0 and beyond.

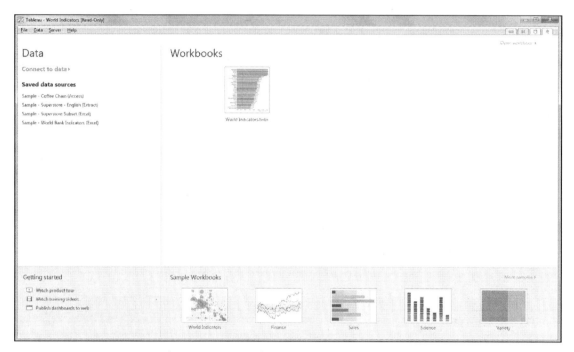

FIGURE 16: WELCOME SCREEN (EARLIER VERSIONS)

WORKED EXAMPLE: CONNECTING TO DATA

Let's create a new data source. For this example, we will connect to an Excel file.

FIGURE 17: WORKED EXAMPLE - CONNECT TO EXCEL FILE

Click on "Excel" and you will be prompted to select the file you want to use as the data source. Select the file you wish to use as your data source and click open.

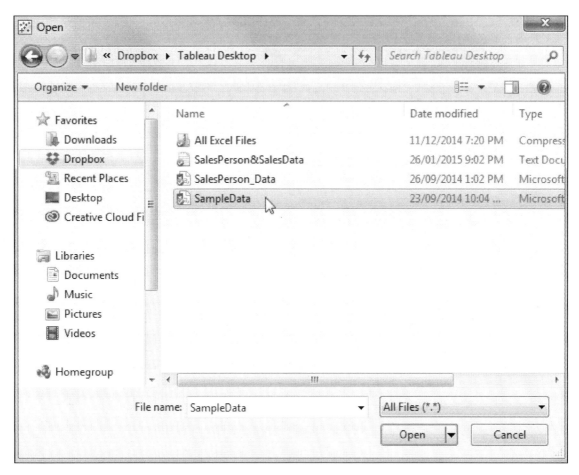

FIGURE 18: WORKED EXAMPLE - OPENING A DATA SOURCE

This takes us to a new screen which is our data source connection screen.

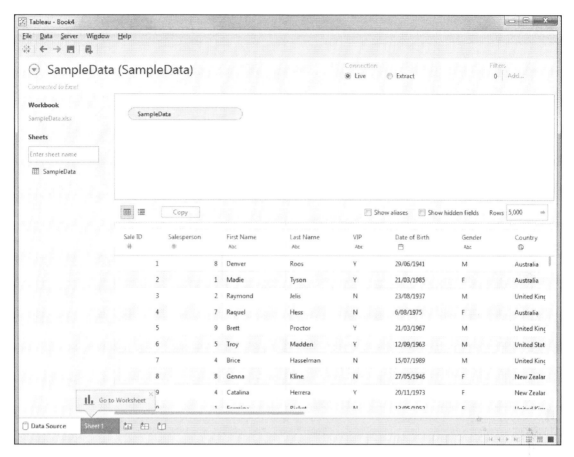

FIGURE 19: WORKED EXAMPLE - DATA SOURCE CONNECTION SCREEN

You will notice on the left of the screen we have the name of the file we have selected to connect to as our data source. If the Excel workbook has multiple tabs, you will see that these have been listed in order as well as sheets. In this example, however, there is only one worksheet within the Excel file so only one sheet has been listed under Sheets — SampleData.

If your excel file has only one worksheet, as in this example, Tableau will automatically use that sheet for the data source. However, if there are multiple worksheets in the Excel file, you will need to tell Tableau which sheet to use. In order to use a specific worksheet within your Excel workbook for your data source, we need to drag and drop the sheet into the top section of this page where it says "Drag Sheets Here".

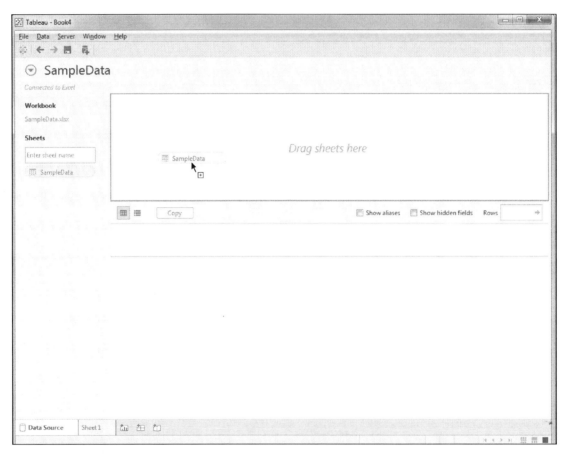

FIGURE 20: WORKED EXAMPLE - DRAGGING AND DROPPING SHEETS

When you do that, you will see that you have the fields and the data from that sheet listed in the bottom half of this page. Here, you can see the type of data that Tableau has recognized inside that file; ABC, indicating a text or string; the hash — or pound symbol — indicating a number; a calendar, indicating a date or timestamp; and other data types that we will discuss later in the book.

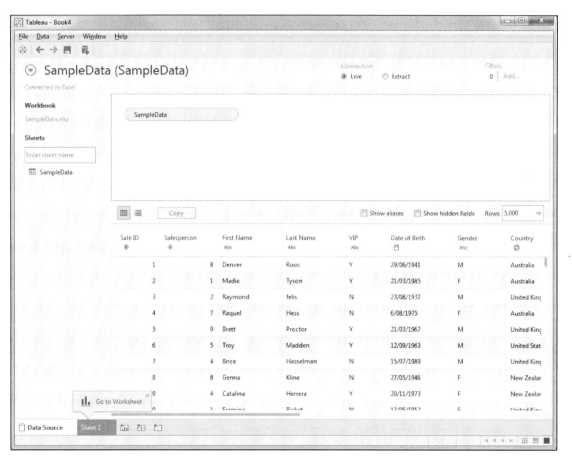

FIGURE 21: WORKED EXAMPLE - WORKSHEET DATA

Once you have successfully connected your data source, it is time to go to the worksheet. To do that, simply click on the dialogue box at the bottom left of screen that says "Go to Worksheet".

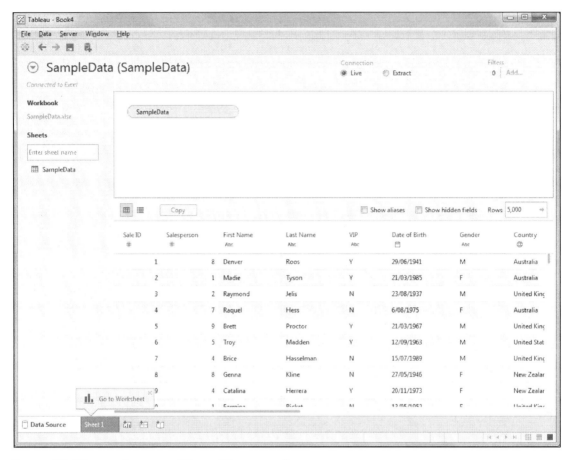

FIGURE 22: WORKED EXAMPLE - "GO TO WORKSHEET"

When we are in the worksheet, we can see a new connection has been created in the data section of our worksheet. In the dimensions, you can see the individual fields that Tableau has identified as our categorization or definition variables. In the measures, you can see the fields Tableau has recognized as numerical fields the way we would want to perform a function on.

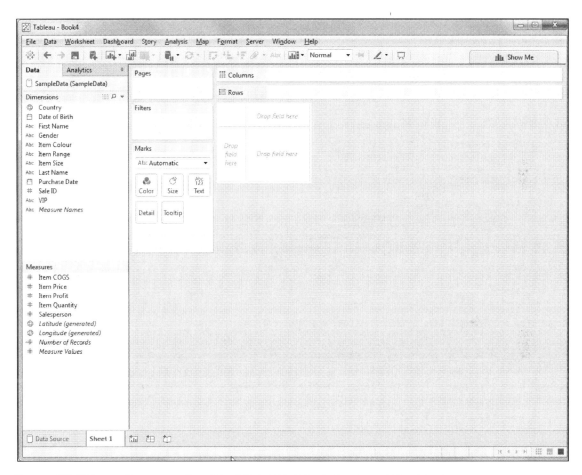

FIGURE 23: WORKED EXAMPLE - CATEGORIZATION VARIABLES AND NUMERICAL FIELDS

If any of these are incorrect, simply drag and drop the field that should be a dimension or measure to the respective area. For example, if I were to drag the Salesperson field from measures into dimensions, you can see now that that field has become a dimension.

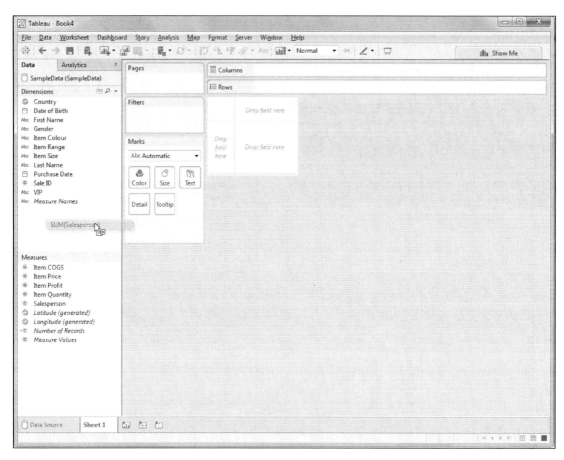

FIGURE 23: WORKED EXAMPLE - CHANGING MEASURES INTO DIMENSIONS

WORKED EXAMPLE: "DRAG AND DROP" DATA CONNECTIONS

Perhaps you've just received an export from your Accounts department that you want to quickly connect to in Tableau and get started on some data exploration. Instead of going through the steps outlined above, you can also "drag and drop" the data file into the Tableau Desktop window.

Simply click and hold your mouse on the file you wish to "drag and drop" into Tableau.

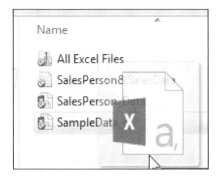

FIGURE 24: WORKED EXAMPLE - DRAG AND DROP DATA CONNECTIONS

Drag the file icon into the Tableau Desktop main window until you see the cursor change to "+ Copy".

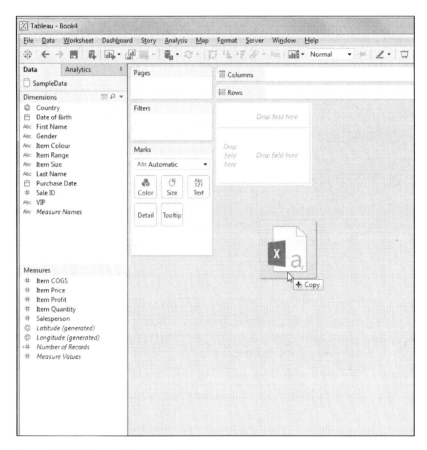

FIGURE 25: WORKED EXAMPLE - COPYING A DATA FILE

Now you can release the mouse and the file will create a new data source within Tableau.

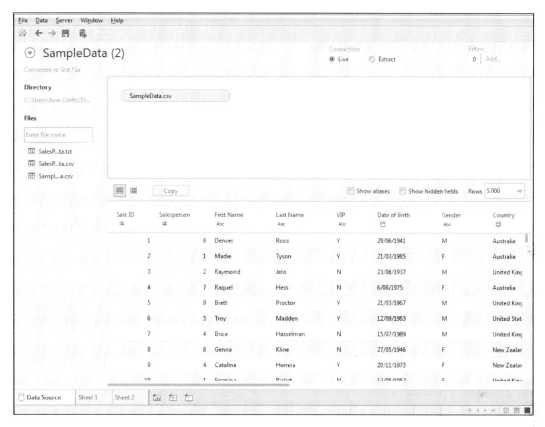

FIGURE 26: WORKED EXAMPLE - CREATING A NEW DATA SOURCE

WORKED EXAMPLE: COPY AND PASTE DATA DIRECTLY INTO TABLEAU DESKTOP

Similar to the "drag and drop" technique outlined above, we can very quickly bring data in to Tableau Desktop without defining a new data source and associated connection by using clipboard functions.

In Microsoft Excel, or any similar program, highlight the data you wish to copy and paste into Tableau. Then, copy this selection to the clipboard.

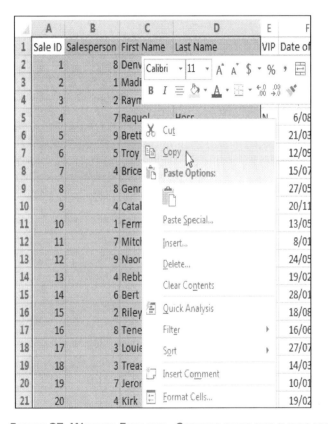

FIGURE 27: WORKED EXAMPLE - COPYING ONTO THE CLIPBOARD

Next, return to Tableau Desktop, go to "Data" on the toolbar, and select "Paste Data".

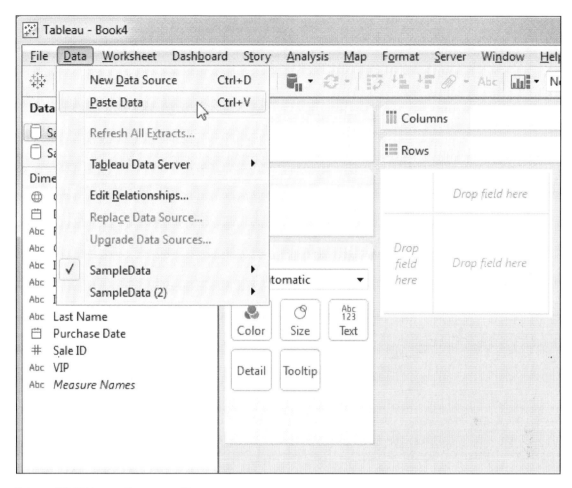

FIGURE 28: WORKED EXAMPLE - PASTING DATA

A new data source will be created from the clipboard and a new worksheet will be displayed with the data you have just copied and pasted into Tableau.

You can also use hotkeys and shortcuts such as CTRL+C (copy) and CTRL+V (paste) to achieve the same result.

3. FORMATTING DATA

There is a beautiful saying that describes perfectly the benefits of investing time in correctly setting up your data sources:

a stitch in time saves nine.

If you are able to make changes to the default settings of each of the dimensions and measures (such as default number formats, default date formats, default sort orders), you will save yourself having to make these changes again and again as you use each dimension and measure in your vizes and dashboards.

Whilst it's by no means compulsory to complete this step, I highly recommend taking the time to structure, shape, and style and sort your data from the outset so that you are not repeatedly making these formatting changes throughout your work. Some of the key formats to consider are:

Numbers

- Whole numbers or decimals?
- Default number format: Currency? Percentage? One or two decimal points?

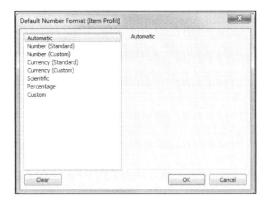

FIGURE 29: NUMBERS

Strings

- Is there a geographic role associated with this field?
- Default sort order?
- Do you want to assign specific colors to different attributes?

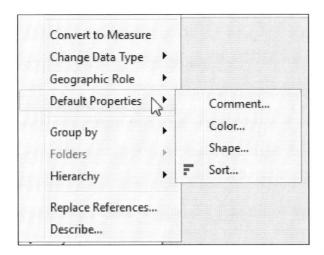

FIGURE 30: STRINGS

As mentioned previously, any changes we make to the formatting, layout or even the contents of our data source do not affect the underlying data. We are working on a framework or a template for our data here, so we are not making any lasting changes to the underlying data.

WORKED EXAMPLE: CHANGING DEFAULT NUMBER FORMATS

Let's start with "**Number of Records**" because this is a field that Tableau automatically generates every time a new data source is created and will be common in every data source you use.

Double click on "Number of Records" to bring that field into the view.

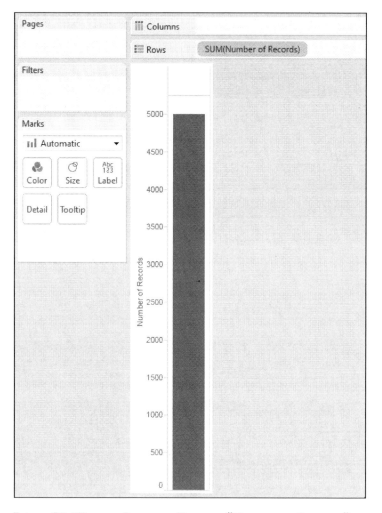

FIGURE 31: WORKED EXAMPLE - VIEWING "NUMBER OF RECORDS" FIELD

This is a good way to get a quick count of the number of rows or records inside the data source. We are going to edit the format of this particular field. In the measures pane, hover over the "Number of Records" measure.

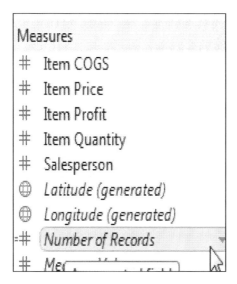

FIGURE 32: WORKED EXAMPLE - NUMBER OF RECORDS MEASURE

Notice the dropdown arrow that appears at the end of the pill. Click this arrow to display a number of helpful tools related to that particular field.

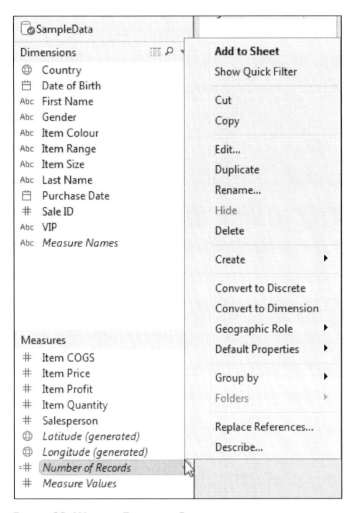

FIGURE 33: WORKED EXAMPLE - DISPLAYING TOOLS

Click on "Default Properties" and you can see the following options: Number Format, Aggregation and Total Using.

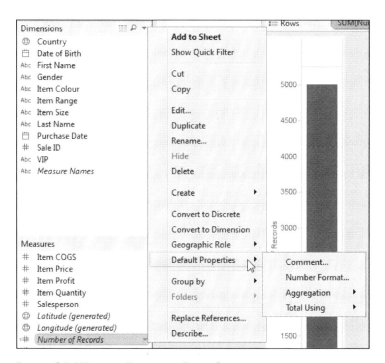

FIGURE 34: WORKED EXAMPLE - FIELD OPTIONS

Let's look at "Number Format" first. Look at the range of number formats available that can be set as the default display for this particular field.

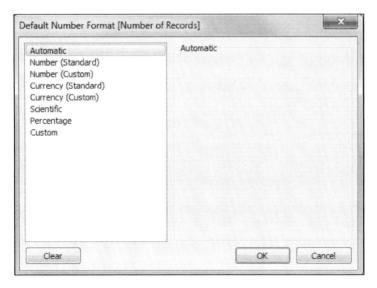

FIGURE 35: WORKED EXAMPLE - NUMBER FORMAT

Because we are expecting this file to have a significant number of records, let's change this particular field's default number format to Number (Custom), with zero decimal places and also set the default display format for this field to units of thousands.

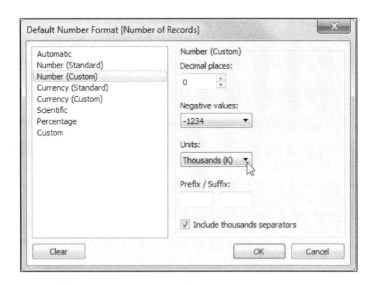

FIGURE 36: WORKED EXAMPLE - CHANGING THE DEFAULT NUMBER FORMAT

Clicking "OK" will return you to the viz. Notice the default number format that we just changed has updated the axis on the bar chart to 1K – 5K. From this point on, any time this field is used throughout all of the visualizations and tables we create, it will now display using the default number format we applied.

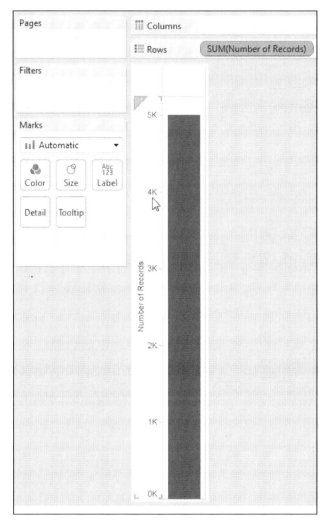

FIGURE 37: WORKED EXAMPLE - DISPLAYING THE DEFAULT NUMBER FORMAT

Familiarity with the underlying data will help us immensely here because we can identify individual measures as having a particular role such as currency or counts. These roles can be embedded in the default properties of the measure so that each time we use them, they will display in the correct format.

WORKED EXAMPLE: CHANGING DEFAULT NUMBER FORMAT TO CURRENCY

By dragging the "Item Price" function into the worksheet, we can see its default numerical format is a simple number format with no decimal places.

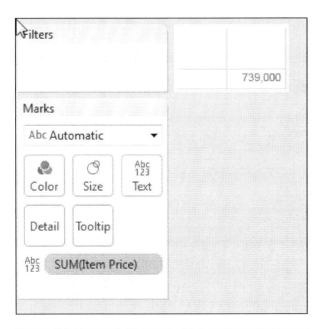

FIGURE 38: WORKED EXAMPLE - SIMPLE NUMBER FORMAT

Perhaps we would like to change this measure to display as a currency value. Click the measure's drop down options, select "Default Properties" and click "Number Format".

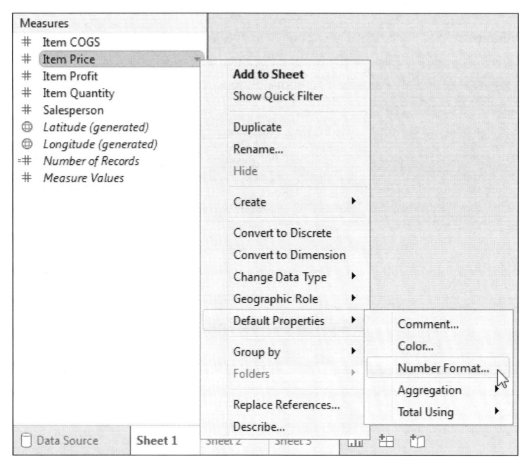

FIGURE 39: WORKED EXAMPLE - NUMBER FORMAT PROPERTY

We'll select the "Number Format" and make this a "Currency".

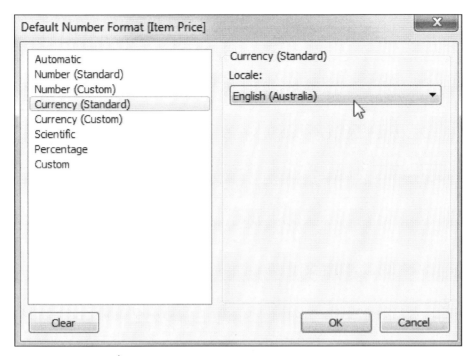

FIGURE 40: WORKED EXAMPLE - CHANGING TO CURRENCY

There is another option here called "Currency (Custom)" where we can say that we don't want to display any decimal places. Additionally, we could set default units of counting to thousands, millions and billions, but because our prices are quite low, we might keep it with "None".

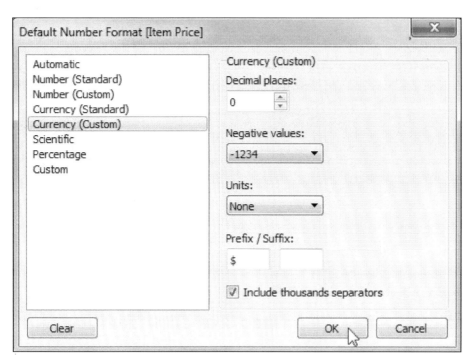

FIGURE 41: WORKED EXAMPLE - CUSTOM CURRENCY

Click "OK" to return to the viz where you will see the dollar sign ($) has been introduced to this field. Any time "Item Price" is used in this workbook it will always display as a currency value with the dollar sign ($) visible.

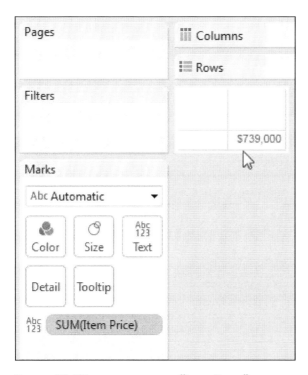

FIGURE 42: WORKED EXAMPLE - "ITEM PRICE" DISPLAY

"Item COGS" (Cost of Goods Sold) is the same story; because this is a cost we can set the default properties to recognize this measure as a currency value. So we go to "Default Properties", then "Number Format"; we can change that to "Currency (Standard)".

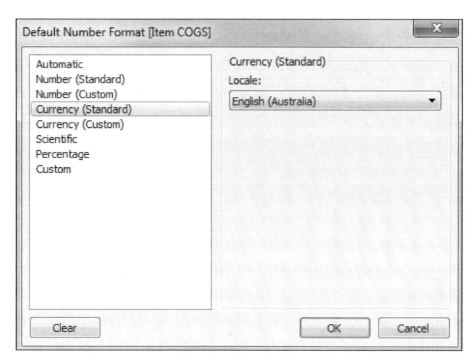

FIGURE 43: WORKED EXAMPLE - CHANGING TO STANDARD CURRENCY

Notice the range of currencies that are available. If I were to select Japanese, see how we now we have the Japanese Yen symbol for our currency value.

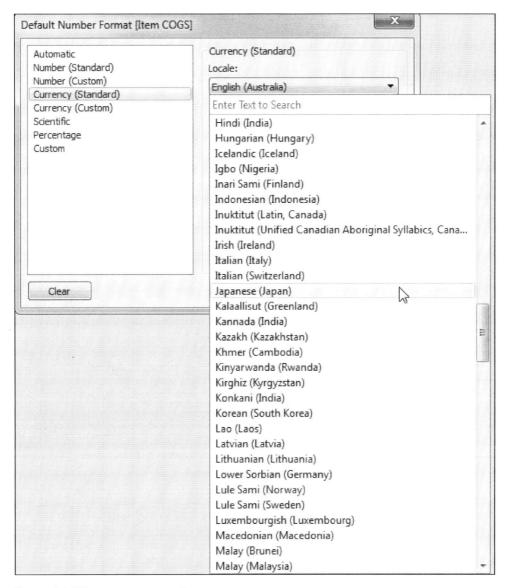

FIGURE 44: WORKED EXAMPLE - RANGE OF CURRENCY

The range of currencies available in Tableau is immense. If you can't find your currency there, you're not trying hard enough!

WORKED EXAMPLE: CHANGING DEFAULT DATE FORMATS

The other items that we might want to change are dimensions such as dates. In this example, we'll change our purchase date — we may want to track sales over financial years as opposed to calendar years.

Double click "Purchase Date" to bring this field into the viz. Alternatively, drag and drop this field onto the column shelf.

FIGURE 45: WORKED EXAMPLE - "PURCHASE DATE" FIELD

Let's expand that to "Quarter" by clicking on the + symbol next to YEAR, and expand further to "Month" by clicking the + symbol next to QUARTER.

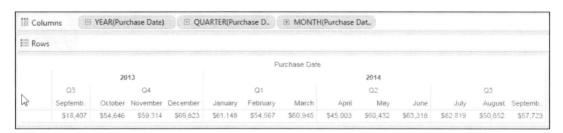

FIGURE 46: WORKED EXAMPLE - EXPANDING DATES

To remove QUARTER from the viz, you can simply drag QUARTER off the column shelf, or you can right mouse click "Quarter" and select "Remove".

FIGURE 47: WORKED EXAMPLE - REMOVING QUARTER

So now we have Calendar Year 2014 showing January through to September, and in Calendar Year 2013, we've got September through to December.

FIGURE 48: WORKED EXAMPLE - CALENDAR YEARS 2013 AND 2014

If we wanted to have a look at these data in a financial year, we can set the beginning of the financial or fiscal year start by going to the Purchase Date's settings, selecting "Default Properties", then "Fiscal Year Start".

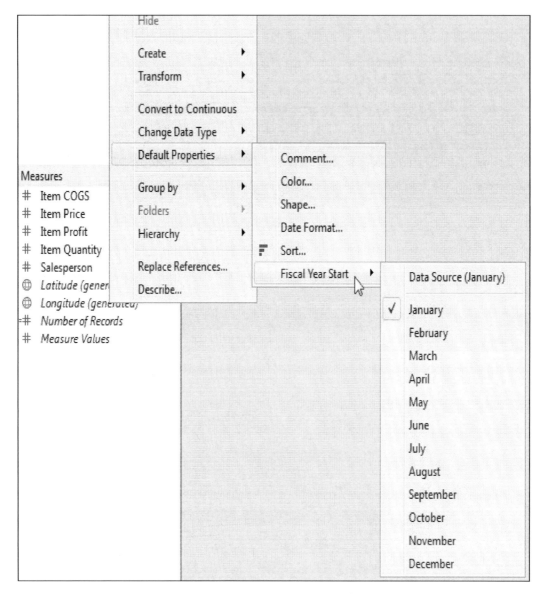

FIGURE 49: WORKED EXAMPLE - SETTING THE BEGINNING OF THE FISCAL YEAR

Let's set the Fiscal Year to start in July. Now look what happens to the worksheet. Notice now how we have a financial year or fiscal year and the data has been re-sorted. So financial Year 2014 ends June and financial year 2015 begins in July.

Columns	YEAR(Purchase Date)	MONTH(Purchase Dat..
Rows		

				Purchase Date								
				FY 2014						FY 2015		
Septemb..	October	November	December	January	February	March	April	May	June	July	August	Septemb..
$18,407	$54,646	$59,314	$69,823	$61,148	$54,567	$60,945	$45,003	$60,432	$63,318	$82,819	$50,852	$57,723

FIGURE 50: WORKED EXAMPLE - SETTING THE START TO JULY

If we were to get rid of MONTH now, we can see that the data has been broken up into financial years as opposed to calendar years.

FIGURE 51: WORKED EXAMPLE - FINANCIAL YEARS

4. BLENDING DATA

I have yet to meet an organization that has perfectly structured, perfectly shaped data with clear relationships between sources. Fortunately, one of the many things Tableau helps us do easily is to blend data sources from different source systems with minimal effort.

Blending data sources can be a tricky skill to come to grips with, but once you have tried and succeeded a few times — you'll be a master blender before you know it!

Basic blending

The easiest and fastest way to blend data sources is on a field that is an exact match across the multiple data sources. Tableau is extremely case sensitive so when we refer to an exact match — it is exactly that. **Exact.** Spelling, spaces, capitalization and punctuation must be exactly the same.

WORKED EXAMPLE: BASIC DATA BLENDING

If there is an exact match in multiple data sources, Tableau will recognize this as a field for blending and give a visual clue of a greyed-out broken chain.

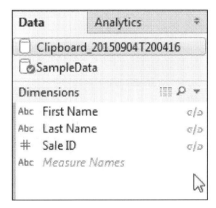

FIGURE 52: WORKED EXAMPLE - BROKEN CHAIN

To 'turn on' the blend, simply click the broken link and the chain will be restored (as indicated by an orange chain). This indicates the blend is active.

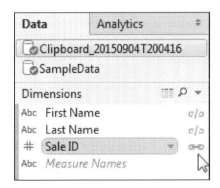

FIGURE 53: WORKED EXAMPLE - LINK RESTORED

You can now use fields from both data sources to build your viz.

Not-so-basic blending

If an exact match is not available, the fastest way to get Tableau to recognize a potential blend is to rename the field you wish to blend with. Let's say the field 'Firstname' in the data source is to be blended with the field 'first name' in the second data source.

Whilst the two field names are similar, they are not an exact match – see the table below for a breakdown of the differences between the two field names:

Primary data source	Secondary data source
"Firstname"	"first name"
Capital F	Lower case f
One word	Two words with space in between

WORKED EXAMPLE: NOT-SO-BASIC DATA BLENDING

Because the two fields are not an exact match, Tableau has not recognized the potential blend and no blend icon is visible.

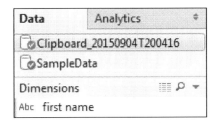

FIGURE 54: WORKED EXAMPLE - NO BLEND ICON

By simply changing the name in the second data source to match the first data source exactly — 'Firstname' — Tableau will take care of the rest.

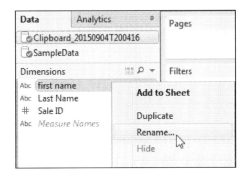

FIGURE 55: WORKED EXAMPLE – RENAMING FIELD NAMES

The field is now available to be used as a blend, as indicated by the broken chain.

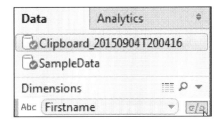

FIGURE 56: WORKED EXAMPLE - BROKEN CHAIN

To turn on the blend, simply click the broken link and the chain will be restored (as indicated by an orange chain). This indicates the blend is active.

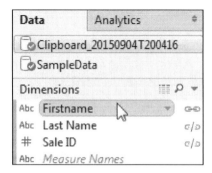

FIGURE 57: WORKED EXAMPLE - TURNING ON THE BLEND

You can now use fields from both data sources to build your viz.

Detailed blending

Of course, there will be times when it is not desirable or feasible to rename fields for the purposes of blending. In these instances we can create custom relationships between data sources.

WORKED EXAMPLE: CUSTOM RELATIONSHIPS

To create custom relationships between data sources, go to "Data" on the toolbar and select "Edit Relationships".

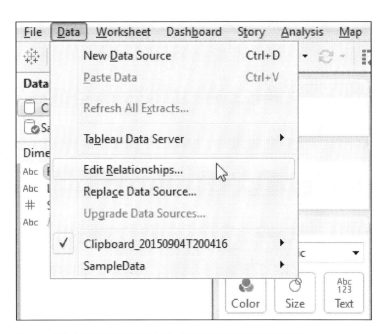

FIGURE 58: WORKED EXAMPLE - EDITING RELATIONSHIPS

Select the primary data source you wish to blend with and then select the secondary data source to be blended. Ensure the custom radio button is selected, and then click "Add".

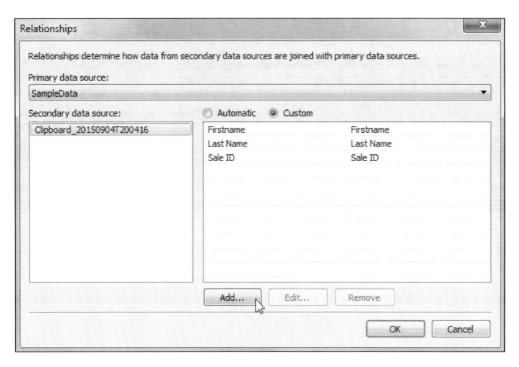

FIGURE 59: WORKED EXAMPLE - SELECTING PRIMARY DATA SOURCE

Here you will be able to select individual fields from the first data source to be blended with an individual field from the secondary data source.

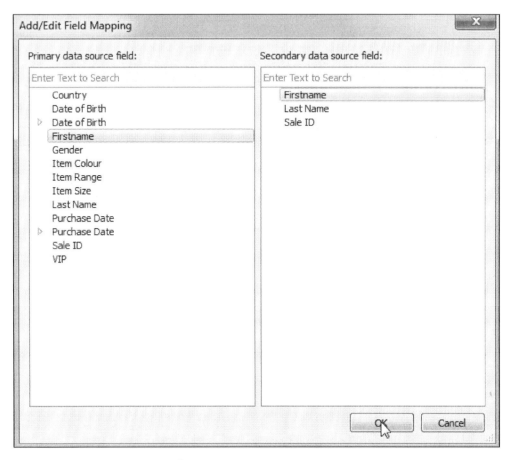

FIGURE 60: WORKED EXAMPLE - SELECTING FIELDS FOR CUSTOM RELATIONSHIPS

This can be repeated again and again to build many relationships.

Note: only fields that are of the same type (string, date, number) will be displayed as available fields when establishing relationship. That is, if a string field is selected from the primary data source, only string fields will be available from the secondary data source.

Once the relationships have been created, these fields will now carry the broken link visual cue, meaning a blend can be turned on as required.

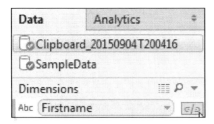

FIGURE 61: WORKED EXAMPLE - READY TO BLEND

To turn on the blend, simply click the broken link and the chain will be restored (as indicated by an orange chain). This indicates the blend is active.

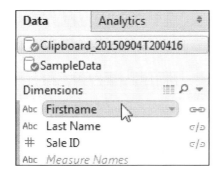

FIGURE 62: WORKED EXAMPLE - ACTIVE BLEND

You can now use fields from both data sources to build your viz.

WORKED EXAMPLE: BLENDING SAMPLE DATA SETS

In our "SalesPerson Data", Tableau has understood "Salesperson" (identified as the hash or pound (#) symbol here) as a numeric field and has identified the field as a measure. It's not a measure though; it is a dimension. Why is it a dimension? Because it is a category or descriptive field, not a field we wish to use in calculations and other numerical functions.

Since "SalesPerson" describes a categorical field, we need to change the field from a measure to a dimension. We can do this by simply dragging and dropping the field from the measures to the dimensions.

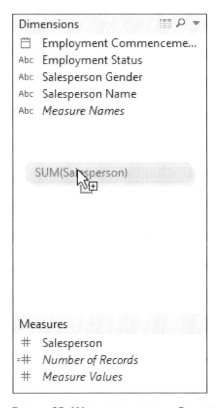

FIGURE 63: WORKED EXAMPLE - CHANGING FROM A MEASURE TO A DIMENSION

Now "Salesperson" can be used as a dimension.

Watch what happens when you bring the salesperson name and salesperson identifier into the worksheet. See this little link to the right of the Salesperson field?

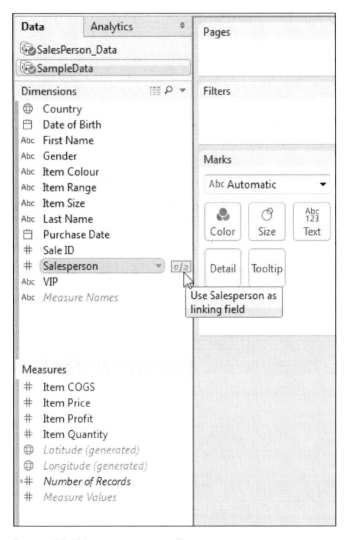

FIGURE 64: WORKED EXAMPLE - ESTABLISHING A LINK

By clicking on this link – turning it from grey to orange – we have established a link between the two data sets based on "Salesperson". We can now blend data from the two data sources.

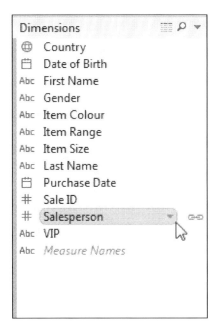

FIGURE 65: WORKED EXAMPLE – FIELD FOR BLENDING

Tableau has determined that "Salesperson" is a common field between the two data sources and can therefore be used as a blending field. Because "Salesperson" has the exact same name (including the capital "S") and is the same data type (numerical) in both data sets, Tableau has identified "Salesperson" as the common field to be used for blending.

Bring in a field from the "Sample Data" (which you remember is a separate data set) to the fields already being used in the view from "SalesPerson Data" – such as "Item Quantity".

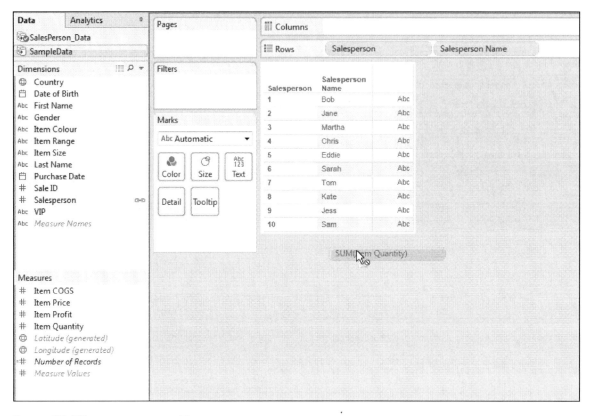

FIGURE 66: WORKED EXAMPLE – USING FIELDS FROM BLENDED DATA SOURCES

We are now able to look at our sales data and our data by salesperson. We've therefore blended data from two data sources, allowing us to have a different view of the data.

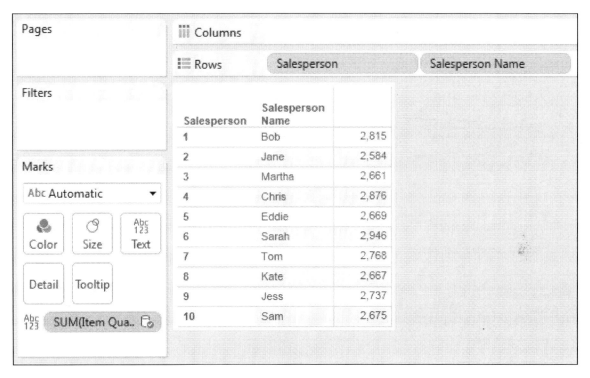

FIGURE 67: WORKED EXAMPLE – TABLE USING FIELDS FROM BLENDED DATA SOURCES

Sometimes, and it often happens, you have a data set that you need to join or blend, and the field names and types are not identical. For example, if we were to rename this field and keep it as "salesperson" rather than "Salesperson" (with the first letter lowercase instead of capitalized), you will see that the option to blend (the 'link') has disappeared.

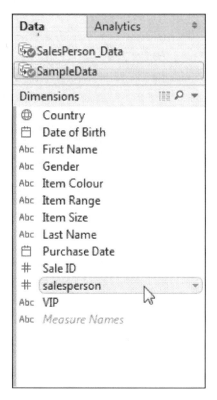

FIGURE 68: WORKED EXAMPLE - DIFFERENT FIELD NAME AND TYPE

As previously mentioned, Tableau will only assume it is a linking field if the format and the name of the field are an identical match.

Let's say we didn't have an identical match, as in this case. We have a lower case field name ("salesperson") in one set and an upper case field name ("Salesperson") in another. We can either rename the field so it is an exact match (i.e. changing the lowercase 's' to an uppercase 'S'), or we can create a custom relationship between the two data sources.

In order to create a custom relationship between the two data sources, click "Data" on the toolbar and then select "Edit Relationships".

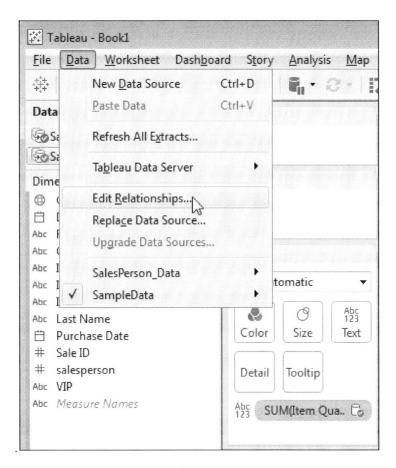

FIGURE 69: WORKED EXAMPLE - CREATING A CUSTOM RELATIONSHIP

Select "Custom".

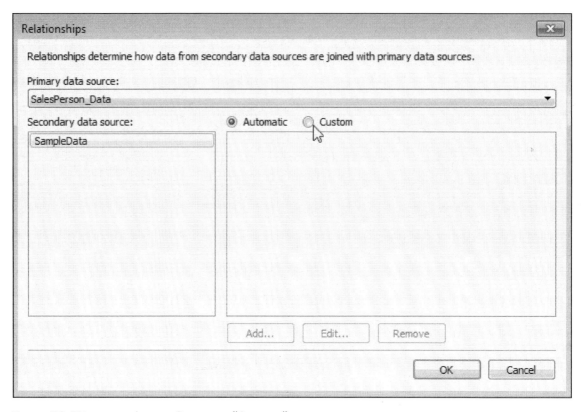

FIGURE 70: WORKED EXAMPLE - SELECTING "CUSTOM"

Then, select "Add" to find the fields we wish to use as our custom relationship.

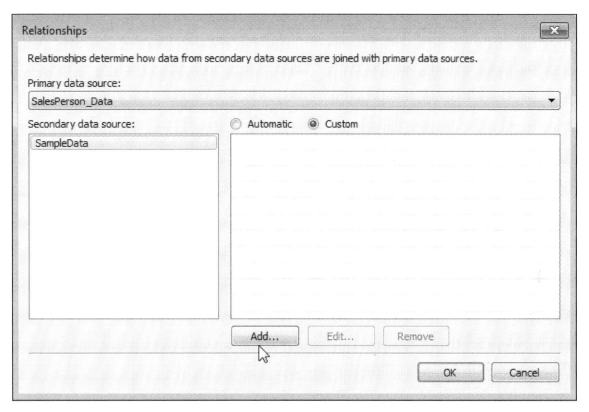

FIGURE 71: WORKED EXAMPLE - FINDING CUSTOM RELATIONSHIP FIELDS

Select the capitalized "Salesperson" field from the primary data source and the lower case "salesperson" field from the secondary data source.

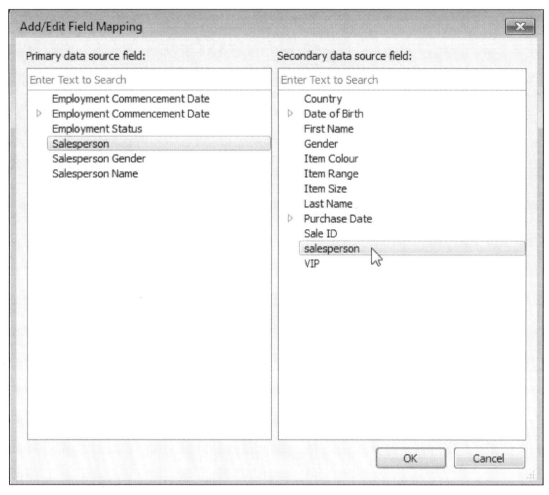

FIGURE 72: WORKED EXAMPLE - SELECTING DIFFERING FIELDS

Click "OK" and you'll see now that our link has returned and the two data sources can again be blended using the Salesperson / salesperson fields.

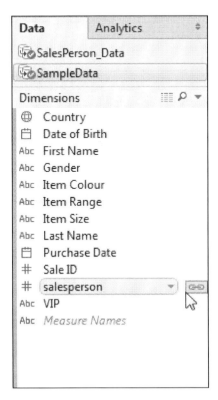

FIGURE 73: WORKED EXAMPLE - LINK RETURNED

5. FIELD NAMES AND ALIASES

As previously discussed, dimensions contain our descriptive or our categorical data. Examples of descriptive or categorical data may include names, places, customer types, product types, employee names, or any other labels or variables you use to define and group your data.

When Tableau brings in the data in for the data source, it brings across whatever attributes or variable names it can find within that data. For example, if we bring a field from the dimensions into the columns shelf, you can see each of the variables that Tableau has picked up from the underlying data.

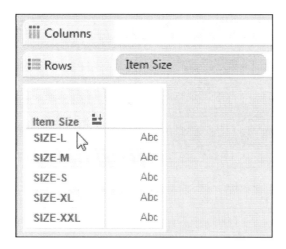

FIGURE 74: VARIABLES WITHIN 'ITEM SIZE' DIMENSION

At any point, we can right mouse click on an individual dimension and select 'Edit Alias' within that dimension.

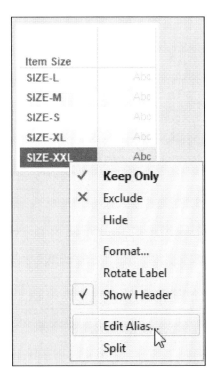

FIGURE 75: EDITING THE ALIAS

Enter the new alias you wish to use

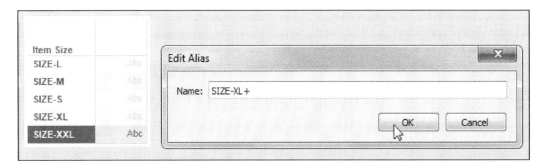

FIGURE 76: ACCEPTING THE ALIAS

You will see the updated alias appear in the viz

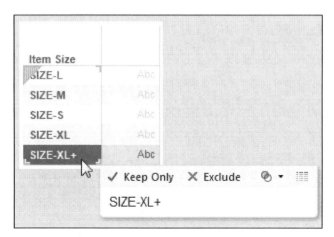

FIGURE 77: VIEWING THE ALIAS

Using an alias can be very helpful when the underlying data has very technical or coded names of variables within fields. For example, if the only data you have access to is a key or index value with some letters to define various variables, you may wish to change the alias to more meaningful terms. Any time you use the field that contains an alias, the alias will then be displayed as opposed to the underlying data value.

WORKED EXAMPLE: IDENTIFYING AND CHANGING ALIASES

To check which fields do and do not have aliases applied to them, you can click on "Data" in the toolbar, select the data source, come down to "Edit Aliases" and choose the field that you wish to check for aliases.

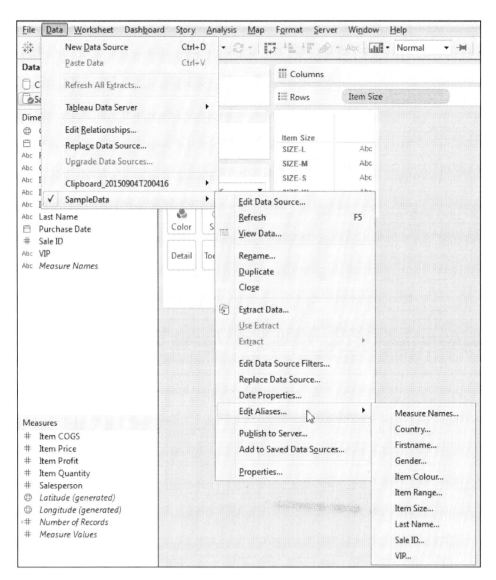

FIGURE 78: WORKED EXAMPLE - CHECKING THE ALIAS

A dialogue box will appear with a table that outlines each of the variables contained within that field and an asterisk indicating that an alias has been set for that member.

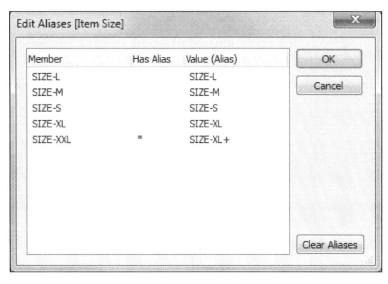

FIGURE 79: WORKED EXAMPLE – EDIT ALIASES

If you wish to clear aliases, you can click "Clear Aliases". You will note that the aliases have been removed from that data source.

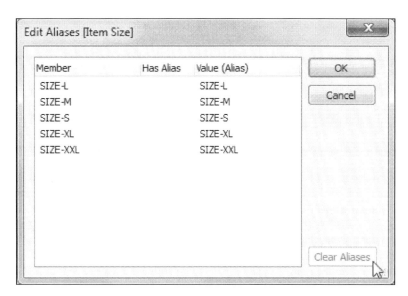

FIGURE 80: WORKED EXAMPLE - CLEARING THE ALIAS

You can also add or edit aliases at this point. To do this, simply click on the label in the "Value (Alias)" column and type the new or changed alias for this member.

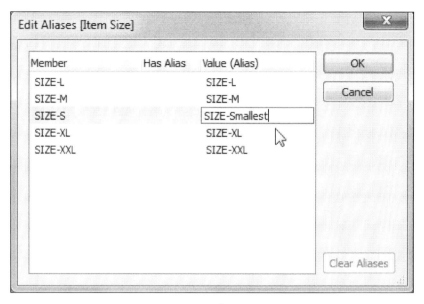

FIGURE 81: WORKED EXAMPLE - ADDING/EDITING THE ALIAS

Click OK to return to the viz – you'll see that the aliases have been updated to reflect the changes made.

FIGURE 82: WORKED EXAMPLE – UPDATED ALIASES IN THE VIZ

6. CALCULATED FIELDS

In addition to the default formats, data path and connection credentials (so that that data can be refreshed), data sources can also hold a number of calculated fields. Calculated fields are fields we create that live in our data source and can be used across multiple vizes and in our dashboards.

There are three ways to create a calculated field. We can either right mouse click in the white section of the dimensions or measures windows and select, "Create Calculated Field".

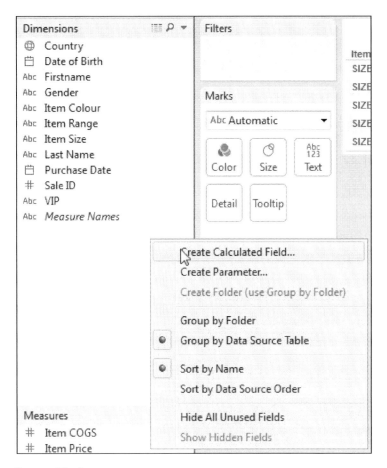

FIGURE 83: CREATING A CALCULATED FIELD

Alternatively, if we know we want to create a calculated field on a particular measure or even a dimension, we can right mouse click on that particular field and say, "Create Calculated Field". This is handy if you know that you have particular calculation that needs to be built on an existing dimension or measure, such as sales volume or a unique identifier as it brings that field into the calculation for you.

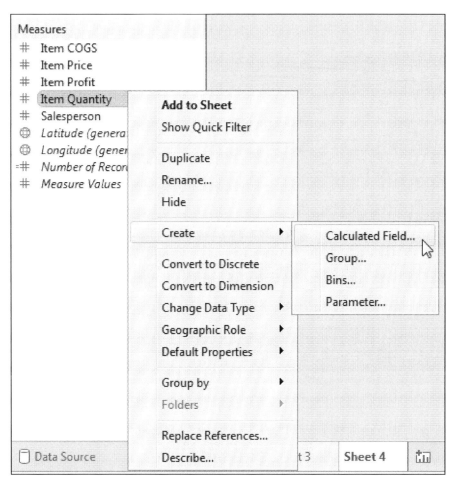

FIGURE 84: CREATING A CALCULATED FIELD ON A PARTICULAR DIMENSION

Either of these options will open a calculated field dialogue box.

FIGURE 85: OPENING A CALCULATED FIELD DIALOGUE BOX

Within the calculated field dialogue box, you will see room for the name of your calculated field, and then also a large section of blank space where we can type our calculation. Over to the right, you will notice an arrow.

FIGURE 86: CALCULATED DIALOGUE BOX AND CALCULATION FIELD

Clicking this arrow will bring up the list of all available functions you can use in your calculated field as well as the associated rule that applies to that type of calculation.

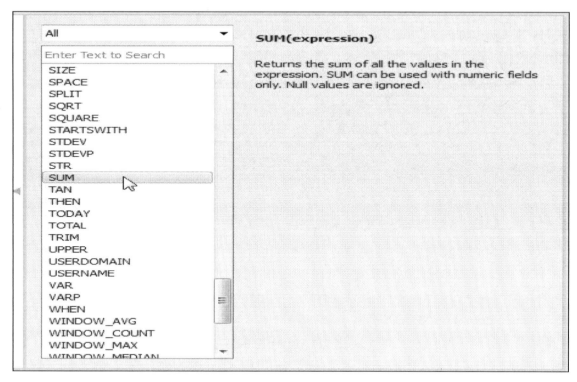

FIGURE 87: AVAILABLE FUNCTIONS

WORKED EXAMPLE: CREATING CALCULATED FIELDS

For example, if I wanted to calculate the difference in date between two dates in my dimensions, I can click on the "DATE DIFF Calculation" and I can see the calculation rules that I need to follow in order to create that calculated field.

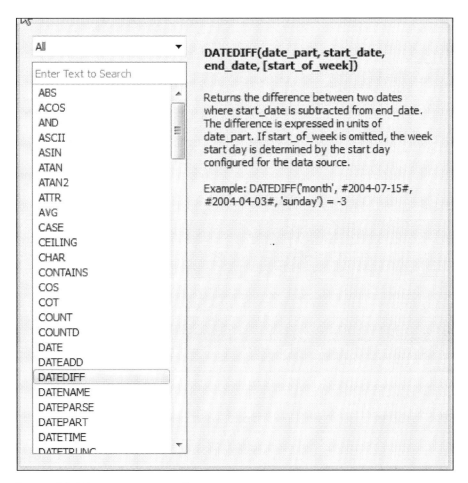

FIGURE 88: WORKED EXAMPLE - CALCULATION RULES

If you are using a version of Tableau Desktop prior to version 9.0, creating a calculated field will look a little bit different. When you create a calculated field you will see the name, a formula window and then a list of fields, parameters and functions that you can use to build your calculation.

FIGURE 89: WORKED EXAMPLE - CALCULATION FIELDS IN EARLIER RELEASES

In version 9.0 and beyond, instead of having a list of available fields, you can simply start typing the name of a field that you would wish to use. Any related fields will become available in a drop down box.

FIGURE 90: WORKED EXAMPLE – TYPE IN FIELD NAMES

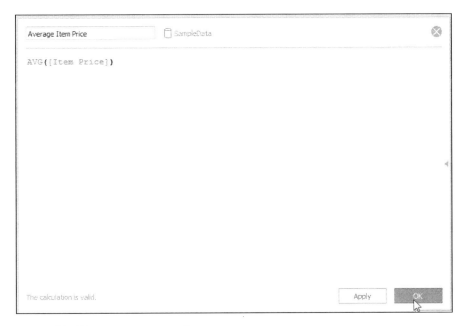

FIGURE 91: WORKED EXAMPLE – SELECT SUGGESTED FIELD NAMES

Once you click "OK", you will see that your calculated field has now become a measure that you can drag and drop or double click to bring into your visualization. You can now use your calculated field as you would any other measure.

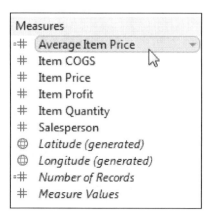

FIGURE 92: WORKED EXAMPLE - CALCULATION FIELD AS MEASURE

Additionally, in version 9.0 and beyond, calculations can be written directly on the column or row shelf. Simply click on the column or row shelf and begin typing your calculated field.

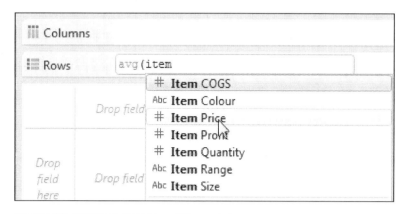

FIGURE 93: WORKED EXAMPLE - WRITING ON THE COLUMN OR ROW SHELF

7. SAVING AND SHARING DATA SOURCES

Now that you have created and made relevant changes to your data source, such as formatting, setting defaults and adding calculated fields, you can save and share this data source. This will save you from needing to reformat and re-customize the data source when you come to use it in future projects.

Publishing to Server

Publishing to Server is, of course, only available if you have a running version of Tableau Server installed. If you do not have Tableau server, you could still create a saved data source which could be put on a shared network drive or emailed to colleagues to allow them to access data sources.

WORKED EXAMPLE: PUBLISHING TO SERVER

To publish a data source to the Server, right mouse click the data source name and select "Publish to Server".

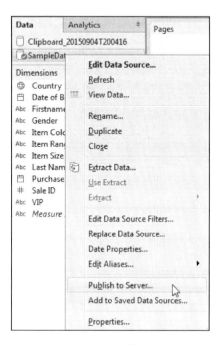

FIGURE 94: SELECTING "PUBLISH TO SERVER"

You will be prompted for your server credentials. Enter these and click "Sign In".

FIGURE 95: LOGIN CREDENTIALS

You will be presented with the dialogue box to publish.

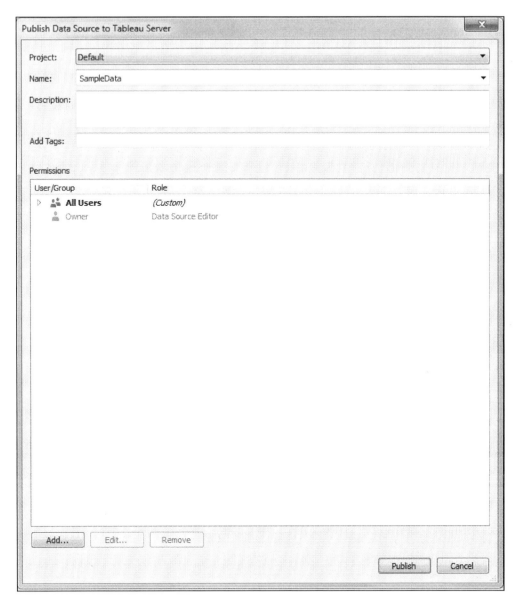

FIGURE 96: "PUBLISH" DIALOGUE BOX

Once a data source has been published to the server, it is available as a Tableau Server data source. To access a data source that has been published to the server, go to "Data" in the toolbar and select "New Data Source".

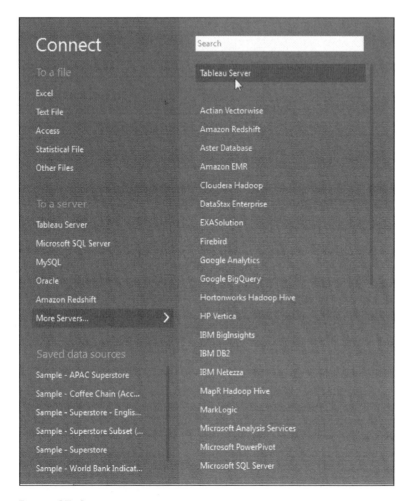

FIGURE 97: SELECTING A NEW DATA SOURCE

Under the "Server" data type connectors, select "Tableau Server". This will be the first option listed.

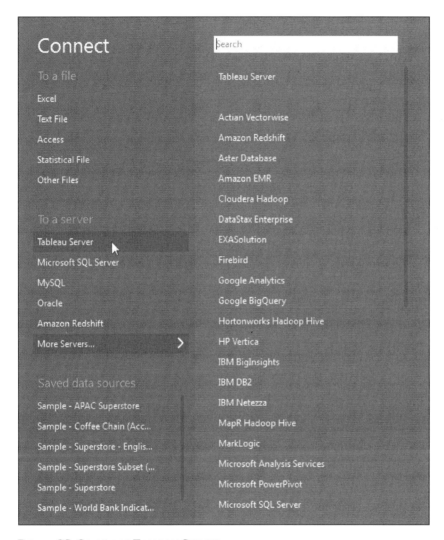

FIGURE 98: SELECTING TABLEAU SERVER

Here you will be prompted to enter your login credentials to Tableau Server.

Once you have entered these and signed in, you will see your new data source that has been published to the server.

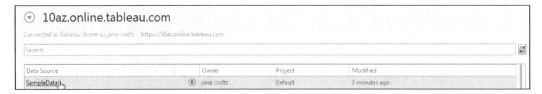

FIGURE 99: PUBLISHED TO THE SERVER

Connect to this data source and you will see a new data source listed in the data pane.

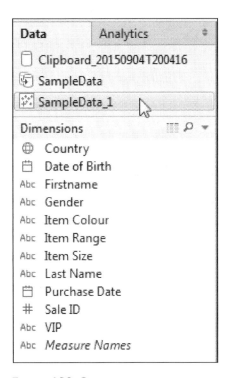

FIGURE 100: CONNECT TO THE DATA SOURCE

All of the changes and formatting that you added to the data source will have been published to the server and available for use in this new data source.

WORKED EXAMPLE: SHARE DATA SOURCES ON SHARED DRIVES

Not all organizations have access to Tableau Server – however this doesn't mean that a beautifully crafted data source cannot be shared and enjoyed by many!

To make the data source available to share by email or on a shared network folder, right mouse click and say "Add to Saved Data Sources".

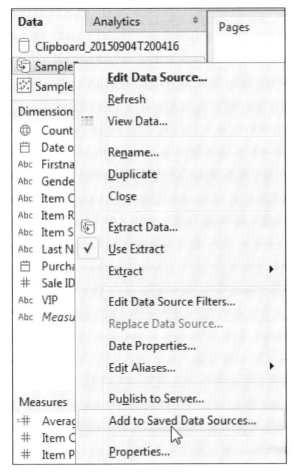

FIGURE 101: ADD TO SAVED DATA SOURCES

You will then be prompted for a location to save your data source.

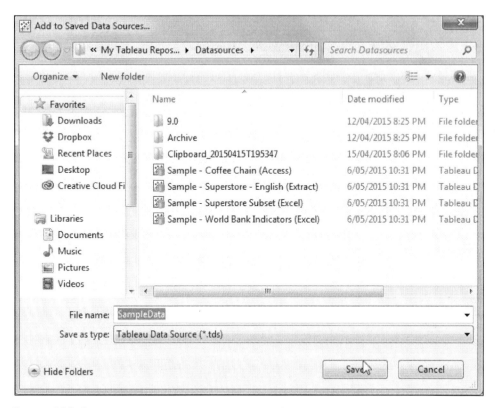

FIGURE 102: SAVE YOUR DATA SOURCE

When you have found an appropriate location for the data source, click "Save" and that data source will saved to your chosen location.

8. EDITING AND REPLACING DATA SOURCES

It's unlikely that you're going to know all the calculated fields, formats and defaults you need for a data source at the time you first create that data source. You may also need to update a data source with the latest data or point the data source connection to a different source.

Don't panic! It's easy to edit — and even replace — data sources at any stage.

WORKED EXAMPLE: EDITING EXISTING DATA SOURCES

To edit a data source, right mouse click on the data source and select "Edit Data Source".

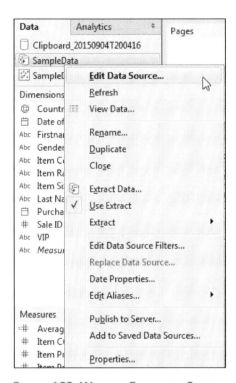

FIGURE 103: WORKED EXAMPLE - SELECTING "EDIT DATA SOURCE", METHOD 1

Alternatively, go to "Data" on the toolbar, select the name of the data source you wish to edit, and then select "Edit Data Source".

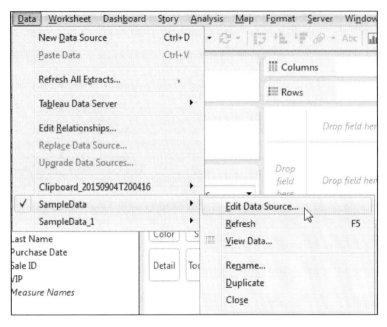

FIGURE 104: WORKED EXAMPLE - SELECTING "EDIT DATA SOURCE", METHOD 2

From here, you can make changes to the individual field types, hide unused fields, unhide fields that do need to be exposed in the data source, and also decide whether you use an extract of that data source or whether you have a live connection.

Creating and using extracts is discussed in more detail in later sections, however here are some basic considerations for deciding whether to use a live connection or use an extract:

Live connections should be used for:

- Data that updates frequently (i.e. stock prices) and needs to be visualized instantly

- Enterprise systems such as multidimensional databases or cubes which are unable to be extracted

Extracts should be used for:

- Data that refreshes on a less frequent schedule, such as hourly, daily or even monthly

- Improved performance for dashboards and vizes

- Advanced calculation functions such as MEDIAN and COUNT DISTINCT

- Instances where offline access to data is required

As a general rule of thumb, I like to work with data extracts over live connections. The performance gains are significant and the other benefits outlined above all add up to a strong case for using extracts over live connections wherever possible.

WORKED EXAMPLE: REPLACING EXISTING DATA SOURCES

There may be occasions where you introduce another data source that you later wish to replace an earlier data source with. This is a relatively easy process; simply right mouse click on the data source and select "Replace Data Source"

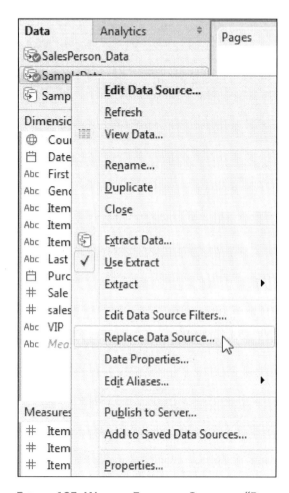

FIGURE 105: WORKED EXAMPLE - SELECTING "REPLACE DATA SOURCE", METHOD 1

Alternatively, select "Data" on the toolbar, click the data source to be replaced, and then select "Replace Data Source".

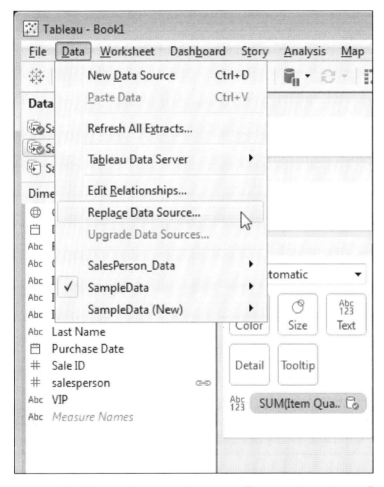

FIGURE 106: WORKED EXAMPLE - SELECTING "REPLACE DATA SOURCE" FROM DATA TOOLBAR

You will then be prompted to select the current data source and the new, replacement data source.

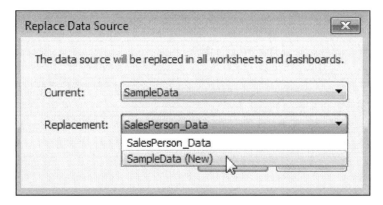

FIGURE 107: WORKED EXAMPLE - FINDING THE NEW, REPLACEMENT DATA SOURCE

Click "OK". Once this process is complete, the dialogue box will close and the replacement will be complete.

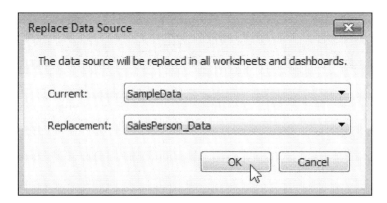

FIGURE 108: WORKED EXAMPLE - COMPLETING THE REPLACEMENT

One of the traps for young players here is that formatting (such as colors and shapes) and aliases may be lost during this stage. This is because the metadata associated with the original data source has been lost. The only way to avoid this is to ensure the replacement data source has the exact same structure and metadata as the original data source.

WORKED EXAMPLE: WORKING WITH METADATA

Let's say our first data source had three fields: name, age and gender. Within the name field there were 5 or 6 first names, all strings; within the age field there were a range of ages, all numbers; and the gender field held either 'male' or 'female' — all strings. Our second data source has the same three fields; however, the age field contains a series of age groups as strings, and gender is defined as either '1' for Male or '2' for Female.

If we replace the first data source with the second data source, we might reasonably expect that our dashboards and vizes would update to reflect the new data. We may have had a color palette defined for gender and also a default order for the display of ages. When Tableau first uses the new data source, it sees that the structure and metadata of the first field ('name') has not changed; however, the structure and metadata of other two fields are not an exact match to the original data source. Tableau then thinks, "These fields must therefore be new and new fields deserve new colors (and shapes)!" and creates new color (and shape) palettes while disregarding the palettes you defined when the first data source was used.

Let's say that the second data source was an identical match in terms of structure and metadata (the age field contained numbers and the gender field contained 'male' and 'female'). After replacing the original data source with the second data source, Tableau recognizes that the structure and metadata of all fields are the same as the original data source, so your original palettes are maintained.

9. USING EXTRACTS

You may have noticed that when you were first creating your data source you were given the option creating an extract or using a live connection. By creating an extract you are essentially bringing in all of the data that meets your filters and indexing this in a way that Tableau has been optimized to use.

The key benefit of using a data extract is speed. No matter how big or small your data, creating and then using an extract as opposed to a live connection will always give you faster performance. The main drawback of using an extract is that it is an extract, i.e. it is not going to update and automatically refresh unless you specify the requirements for it to do so.

WORKED EXAMPLE: CREATING AN EXTRACT

If you did not already create an extract via the data connection screen, right mouse click on the data source and select "Extract Data". Here you will be provided with a dialogue box where you can add filters and conditions to your extract. You can also set the type of extract, whether that is a full refresh or an incremental refresh of the data so that the extract is refreshed.

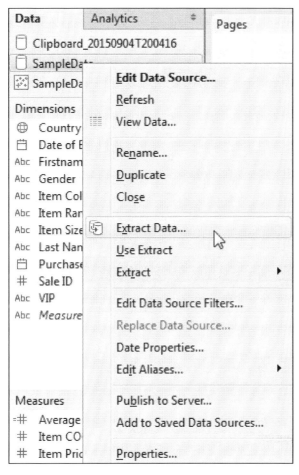

FIGURE 109: WORKED EXAMPLE - SELECTING "EXTRACT DATA"

To start, simply create an extract with no filters, no aggregation and the number of rows set as "All rows", which means each time the extract will be refreshed.

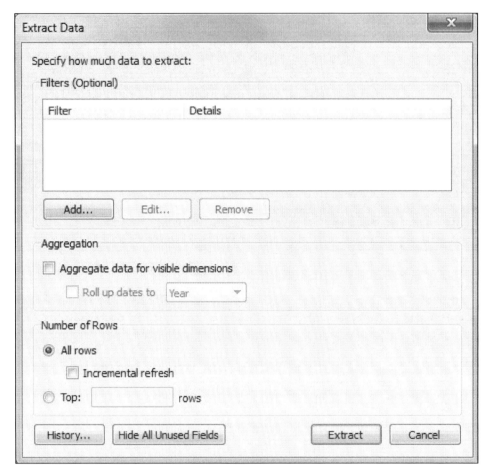

FIGURE 110: WORKED EXAMPLE - STARTING THE EXTRACT

Click "Extract" and the extract process will begin. Selecting "Extract Data" creates a Tableau Data Extract (identified by the abbreviation .tde). This is indicated by an extract icon next to the data source name.

FIGURE 111: WORKED EXAMPLE - EXTRACT ICON

A word of caution: if you're dealing with a significantly sized data set, such as millions of rows, or into gigabits as opposed to kilobits or megabits, creating an extract will take some time. However, as mentioned previously, the benefit of using an extract, particularly when you are dealing with significantly sized data set, is performance. While it may take some time to generate the extract, you will notice a significant boost in your viz performance when using this extract instead of a live connection as the extracting process imports the data through the Tableau Date Engine which vastly improves the speed of queries..

WORKED EXAMPLE: AUTOMATICALLY REFRESHING EXTRACTS

In order to set an extract refresh schedule, you first need to create a packaged workbook, which will then allow you to save and publish the embedded extract to Tableau Server. To do this, go to the file menu, select "Save As". Save it as the file type Tableau Packaged Workbook (*.twbx), then click "Save".

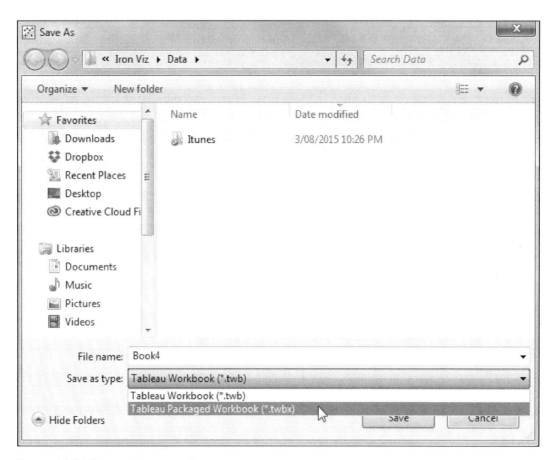

FIGURE 112: WORKED EXAMPLE - SAVING AN EMBEDDED EXTRACT

Alternatively, you can go to the file menu, click "Export Packaged Workbook", choose the location and select "Save".

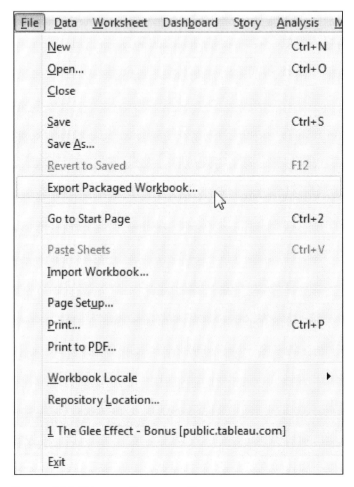

FIGURE 113: WORKED EXAMPLE - EXPORT PACKAGED WORKBOOK

Once you have done this we can publish this packaged workbook to the server. To publish, click on "Server" and select "Publish Workbook".

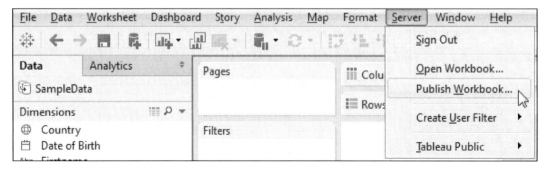

FIGURE 114: WORKED EXAMPLE - "PUBLISH WORKBOOK"

You will be prompted with login credentials if you have not already logged into the server. Select the project where you wish to publish your workbook.

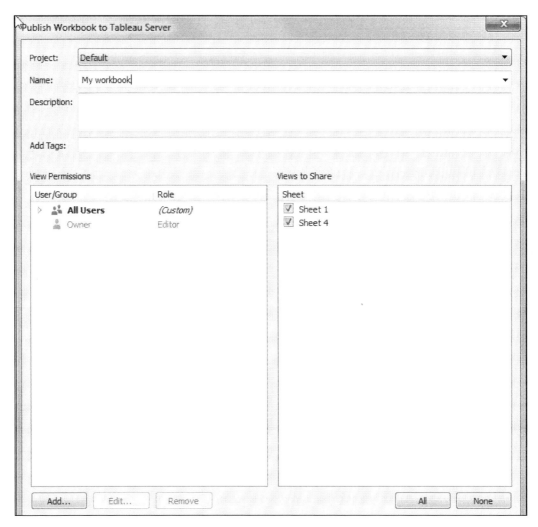

FIGURE 115: WORKED EXAMPLE - SELECT PUBLICATION SOURCE

At the bottom of this dialogue box, you will see a "Scheduling and Authentication" button.

FIGURE 116: WORKED EXAMPLE - "SCHEDULING AND AUTHENTICATION"

Click this and you will be presented with another dialogue box where you can set the refresh schedule for the extract.

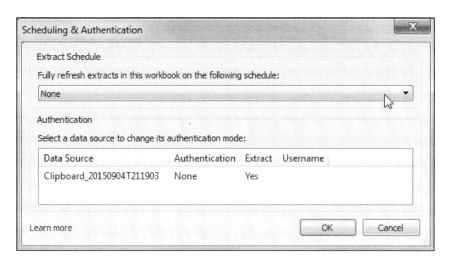

FIGURE 117: WORKED EXAMPLE - SET THE REFRESHING SCHEDULE

The extract schedule that you set should be based on the content of the data. For example, if you have data that needs to be refreshed on a regular basis as it changes frequently, you may find the fifteen minute refresh more suits your needs. However, if the data that you are setting to refresh is only updated on irregular basis or less frequently, such as at the end of the month, you can designate it to update after a longer duration, such as weekly or monthly.

If it is a large data source, I also suggest setting the refresh to occur either early mornings or over the weekend.

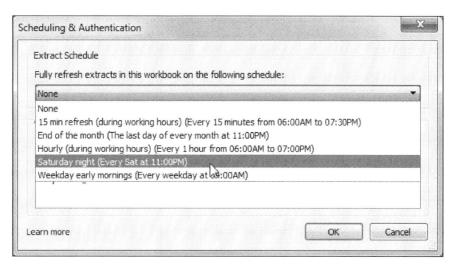

FIGURE 118: WORKED EXAMPLE - FINDING THE RIGHT SCHEDULE

Make sure that the dialogue box has an embedded password set for any extracts that you wish to automatically refresh.

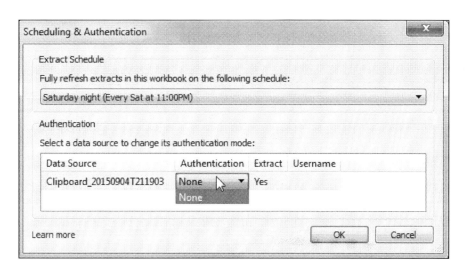

FIGURE 119: WORKED EXAMPLE - EMBEDDED PASSWORDS

Click OK, then "Publish" You will find that your extract has been published to the server and will now automatically refresh based on the schedule that you have set.

DETAILS

Congratulations — you've made it through the data phase! Now it's time to have some fun, explore the more exciting capabilities of Tableau Desktop and build some amazing visualizations!

There are a few staples of data visualization:

- Bar and line charts
- Pie charts
- Geographic maps
- Scatter plots
- Tables and crosstabs

Each of these staples is covered in the sections below.

1. BAR & LINE CHARTS

Whilst probably the most simple of visualization capabilities, bar and line charts are extremely effective for displaying volume and performance over time.

Bar Chart

To create a bar chart you need to have at least one measure available in your data set. Let's use "Number of Records".

WORKED EXAMPLE: CREATING BAR CHARTS

Double click or drag "Number of Records" to the columns shelf.

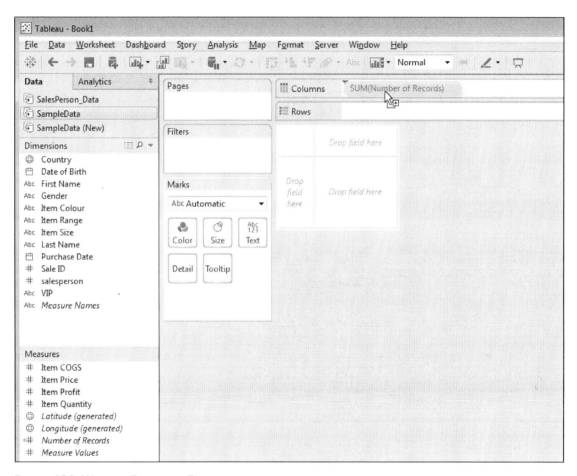

FIGURE 120: WORKED EXAMPLE - BEGINNING YOUR BAR CHART

To split the bar by categories, drag a dimension to the column shelf or double click a dimension.

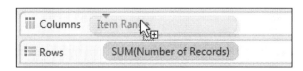

FIGURE 121: WORKED EXAMPLE - SPLITTING THE BAR

Once you have a measure on the row shelf and a dimension on the column shelf, you will be able to see your bar chart.

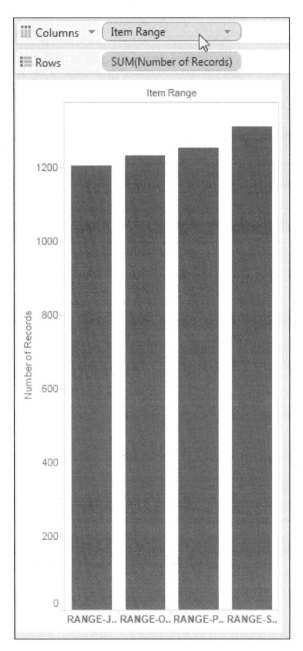

FIGURE 122: WORKED EXAMPLE - VIEWING THE BAR CHART

Let's sort the bar chart by size. You can do this by using the drop down menu from your dimension. Click "Sort".

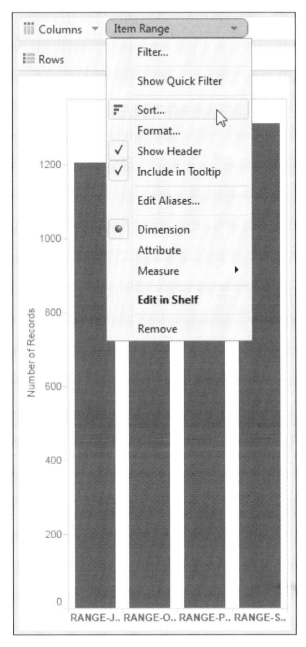

FIGURE 123: WORKED EXAMPLE - SORTING BAR CHART BY SIZE

Now select "Ascending" or "Descending", then use the field, number of records and click "Apply". This sorts your bar chart.

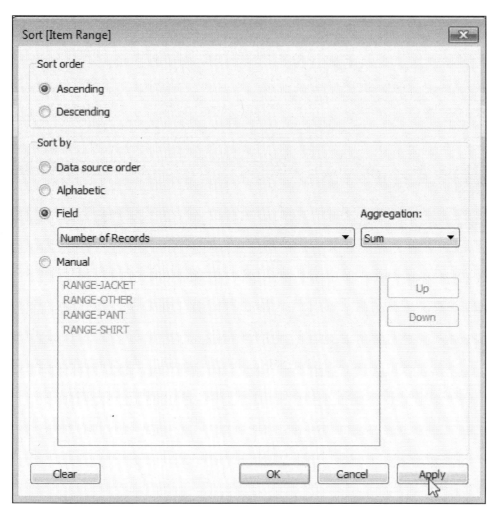

FIGURE 124: WORKED EXAMPLE - SETTING ITEM RANGE

Alternatively, you can hover over the axis and you will be presented with a "sort" icon.

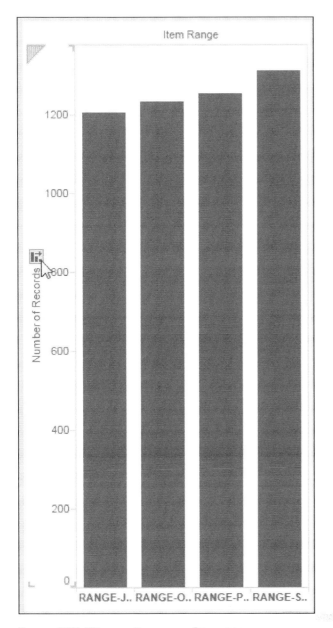

FIGURE 125: WORKED EXAMPLE - SORT ICON

Clicking this icon will change the sort order of the bars.

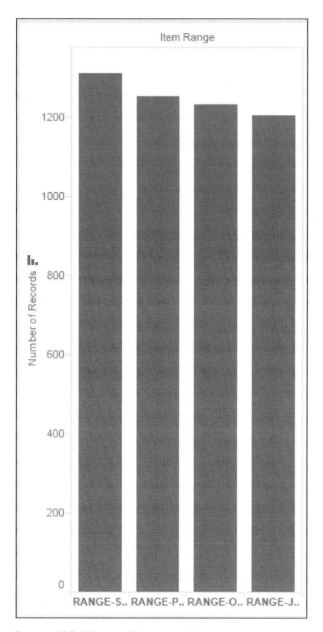

FIGURE 126: WORKED EXAMPLE - CHANGING BAR ORDER

Color can be added to your bar chart using any of the controls on the Marks Card.

Drag the same dimension as is used in our bar chart to the color section of the Marks Card.

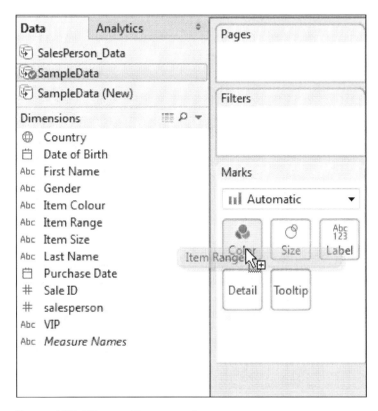

FIGURE 127: WORKED EXAMPLE - ADDING COLOR

The bar chart has now changed and is displaying a different color for each attribute within the Item Range dimension.

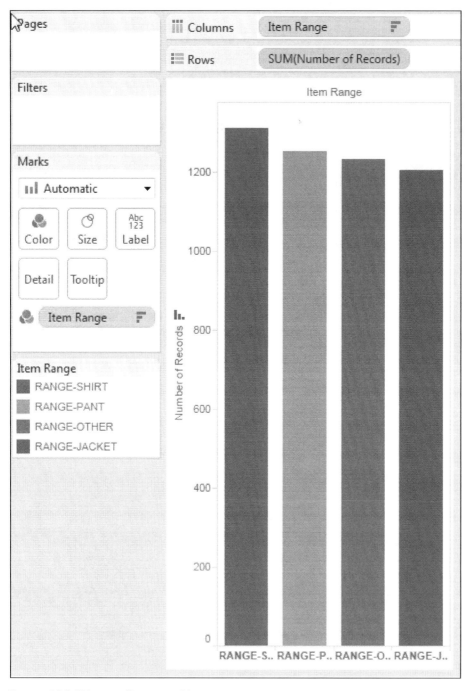

FIGURE 128: WORKED EXAMPLE - VIEWING BAR COLOR

Similarly, you may wish to add the value of each of the bar charts as a label on the chart itself. You can drag and drop the 'Number of Records' measure to the label section of the Marks Card.

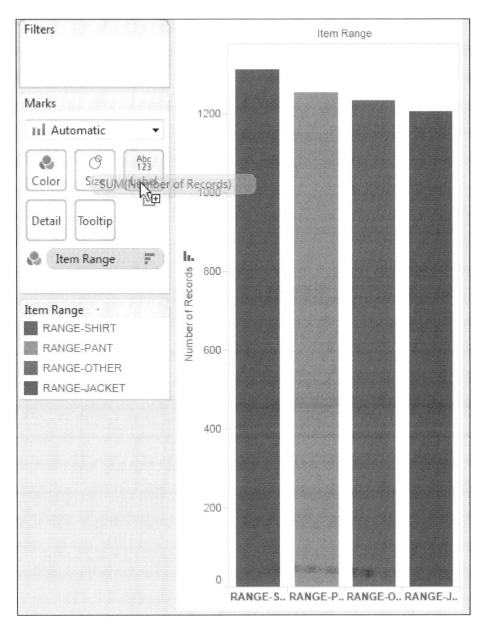

FIGURE 129: WORKED EXAMPLE - ADDING LABELS TO THE BAR CHART

The labels will now appear on your bar chart.

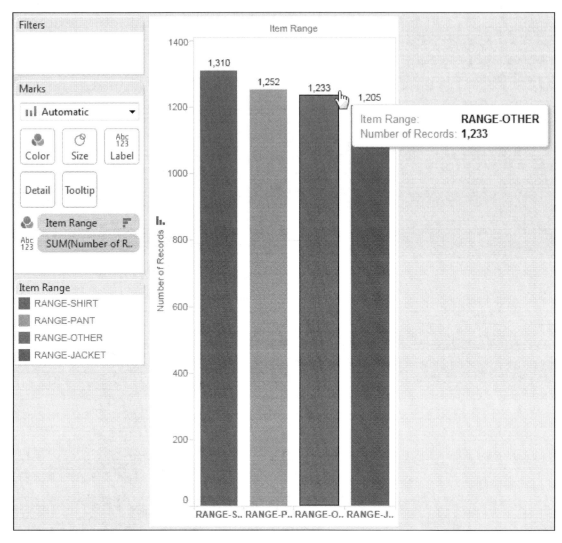

FIGURE 130: WORKED EXAMPLE - VIEWING A LABEL ON THE BAR CHART

Line charts

The process of creating a line chart is exactly the same, except that to create a line chart, we also need at least one date. The reason we need a date to create a line chart is because line charts are our best way of displaying performance over time.

WORKED EXAMPLE: CREATING LINE CHARTS

Double click a date field within your line chart or drag the date field onto the column shelf.

FIGURE 131: WORKED EXAMPLE - CLICKING A DATE FIELD

You can vary the display format of the date by clicking the + icon on the pill to show quarters, months and days.

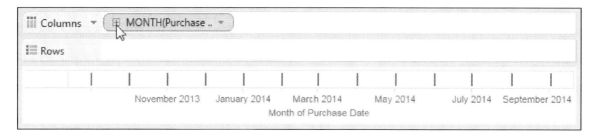

FIGURE 132: WORKED EXAMPLE - VARYING DATE DISPLAY FORMAT

Alternatively, you can use the drop down menu to select a specific date format.

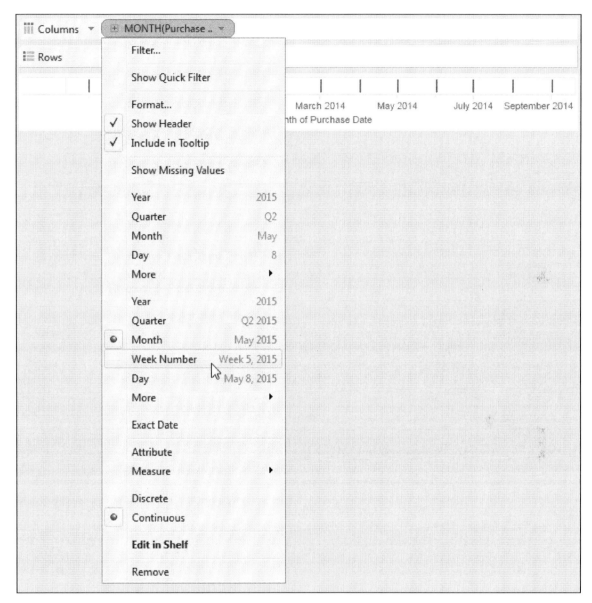

FIGURE 133: WORKED EXAMPLE - SELECTING A SPECIFIC DATE FORMAT

Let's use "Number of Records" again. Double click or drag "Number of Records" to the rows shelf.

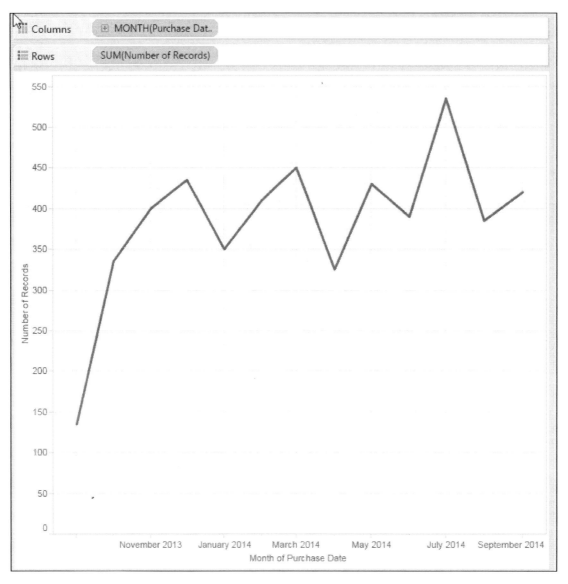

FIGURE 134: WORKED EXAMPLE - BRINGING "NUMBER OF RECORDS" TO THE ROWS SHELF

If you were presented with a table as opposed to a line chart, simply go to the Marks Card and use the drop down menu to select "Line Chart".

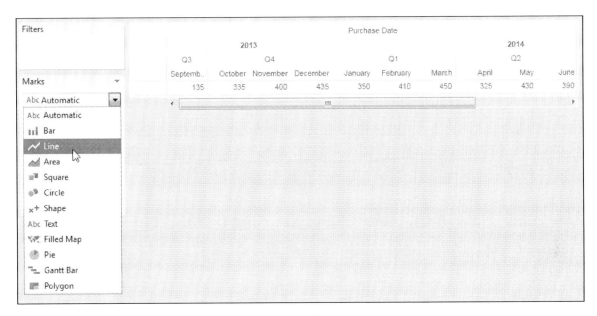

FIGURE 135: WORKED EXAMPLE - SELECTING "LINE CHART"

Then, drag the Number of Records pill to the Rows shelf.

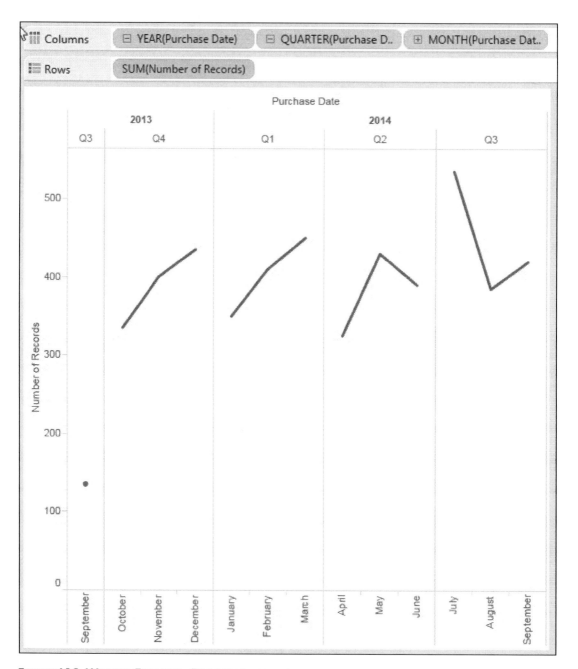

FIGURE 136: WORKED EXAMPLE - DRAGGING A PILL TO THE ROWS SHELF

If your line chart appears in discrete sections — rather than a continuous line — you will need to change your date field to continuous rather than discrete. To do this, use the drop down menu on the date pill and select "Continuous".

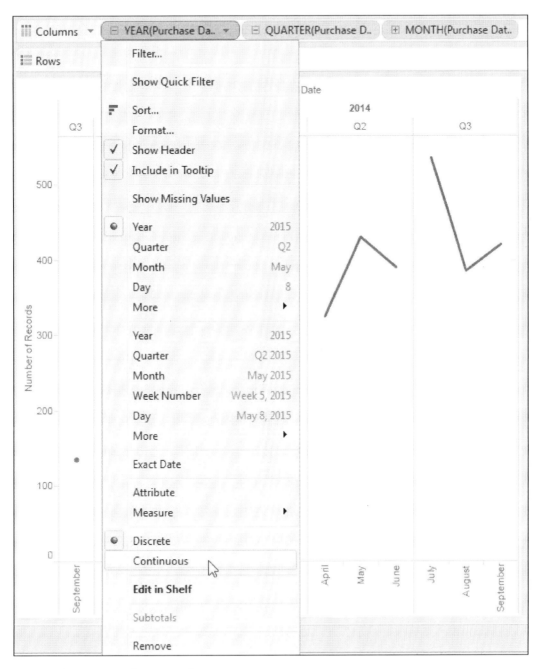

FIGURE 137: WORKED EXAMPLE - CHANGING FROM DISCRETE TO CONTINUOUS

You will notice that the continuous (green) date pill has moved to the end of the column shelf and the discrete (blue) date pills have moved to the front of the shelf.

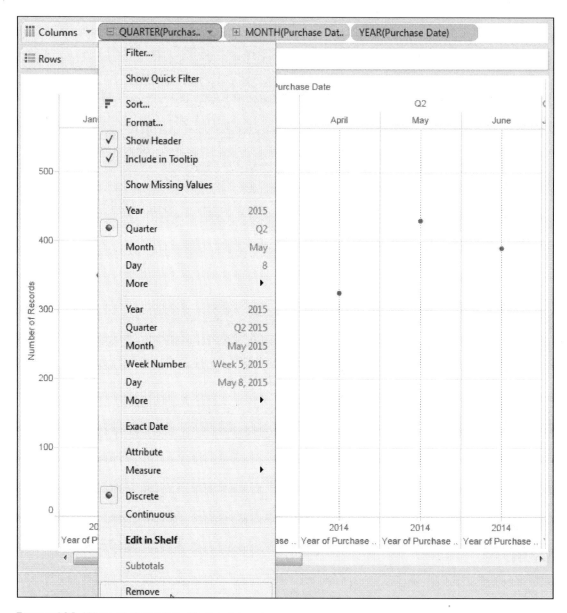

FIGURE 138: WORKED EXAMPLE - CLICKING REMOVE

By clicking "Remove" on the drop down menus associated with these discrete date pills, you will turn your line chart into a continuous time series.

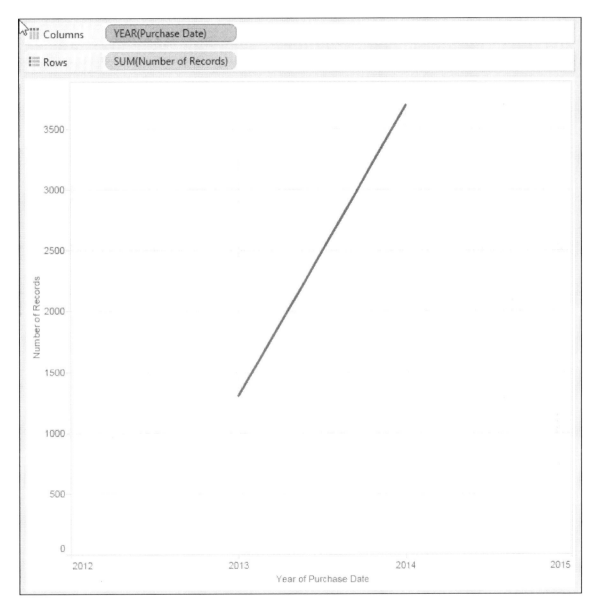

FIGURE 139: WORKED EXAMPLE - CONTINUOUS LINE

You can then add more granularity in the date display format. To do this, go to the drop down menu one more time to select your preferred date format.

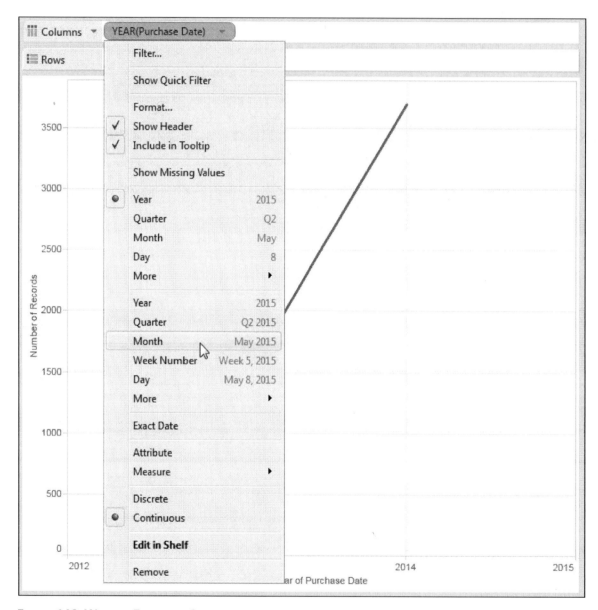

FIGURE 140: WORKED EXAMPLE - SELECTING PREFERRED DATE FORMAT

To disaggregate the line chart, simply drag a dimension onto the detail card or onto the color card.

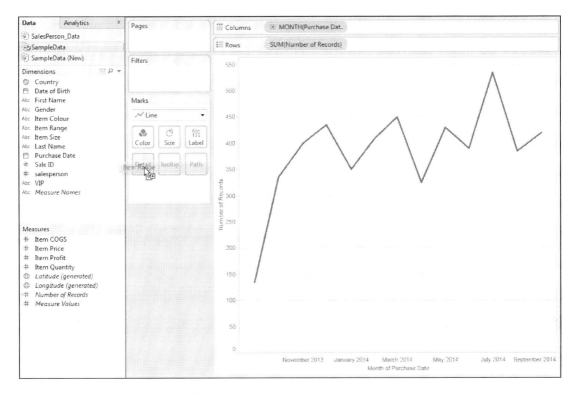

FIGURE 141: WORKED EXAMPLE - DISAGGREGATING THE LINE CHART

Your originally aggregated line will be split into whatever dimension you have added to the viz.

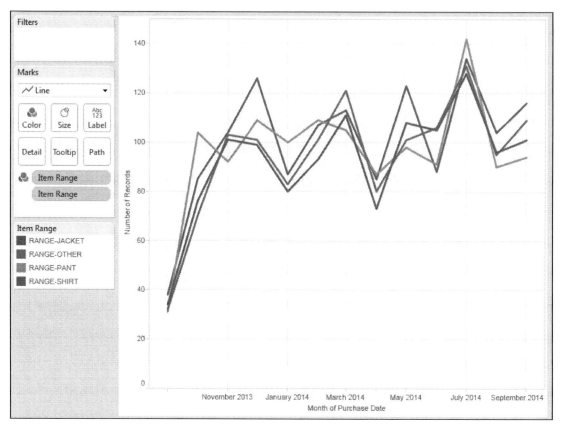

FIGURE 142: WORKED EXAMPLE - FINISHED SPLIT LINE GRAPH

To format any of the axes on the line or bar chart, right mouse click on the axis, then select "Edit Axis".

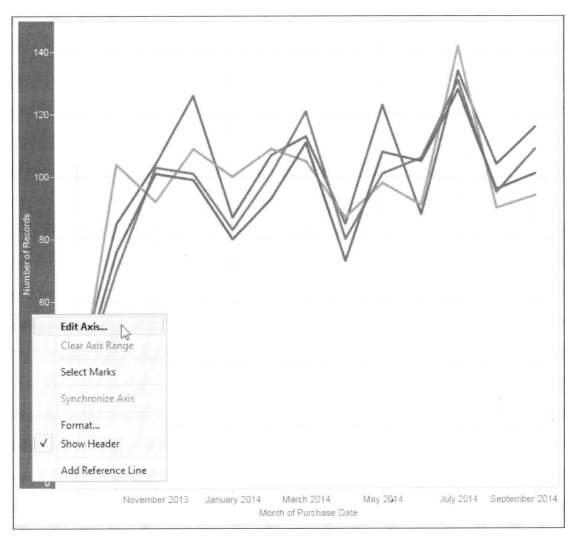

FIGURE 143: WORKED EXAMPLE - EDIT AXIS

Here you can change the presentation and layout of the axis as required.

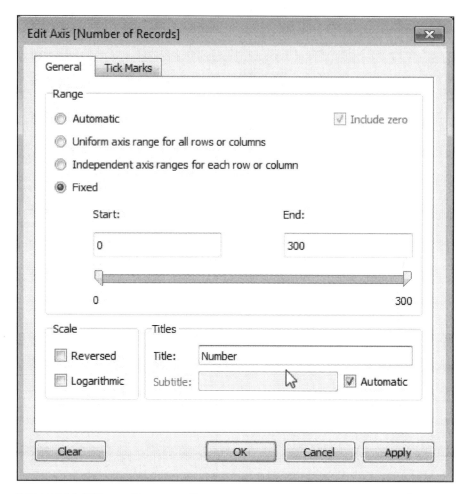

FIGURE 144: WORKED EXAMPLE - CHANGING PRESENTATION AND LAYOUT OF AXIS

2. GEOGRAPHIC MAPS

One of the most popular features of Tableau Desktop is the ability to build geographic maps with only a few clicks. In order to do this we need at least one geographic field inside our data source. Geographic fields are indicated by a globe icon.

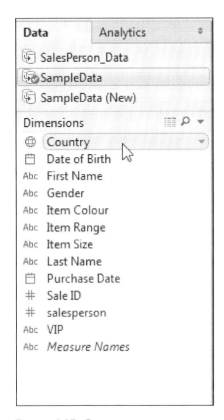

FIGURE 145: GLOBE ICON

WORKED EXAMPLE: CREATING GEOGRAPHIC MAPS

Simply double click a geographic field and your map will be drawn for you.

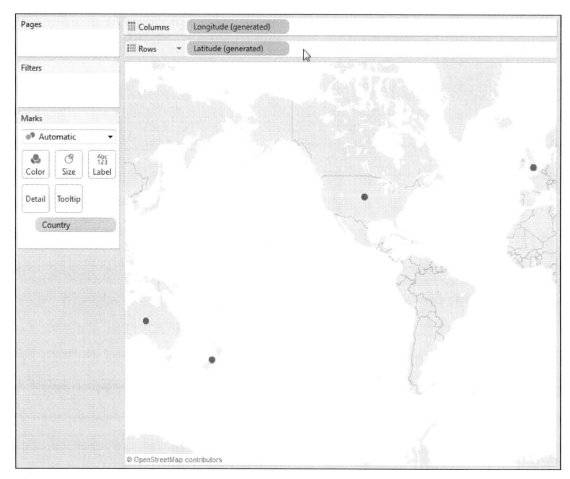

FIGURE 146: WORKED EXAMPLE - DRAWING A MAP

The geographic field you double clicked has moved to the Marks Card and Longitude and Latitude pills have been automatically placed on the Column and Rows shelves.

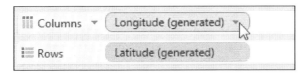

FIGURE 147: WORKED EXAMPLE - LONGITUDE AND LATITUDE

Tableau automatically generates Longitude and Latitude fields whenever these are required (i.e. whenever a geographic field is used in a viz).

From here you can use your measures and dimensions to reflect the story you wish to tell with your data. You can drag measures and dimensions to color, size and shape cards on the marks shelf.

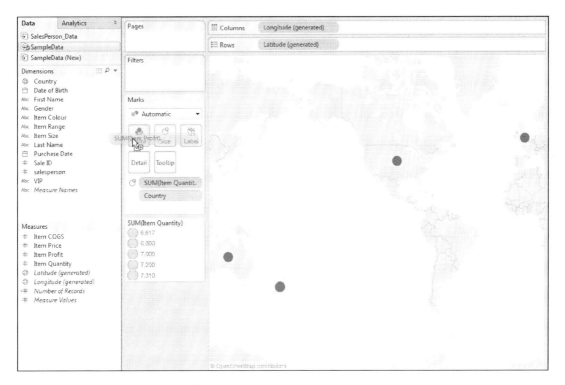

FIGURE 148: WORKED EXAMPLE - SELECTING COLOR, SIZE, AND SHAPE

Let's use size to indicate the number of sales in a country, and we'll use color to show the profitability of a country. Drag Item Quantity to the size section on the Marks Card and drag Item Profit to the color section.

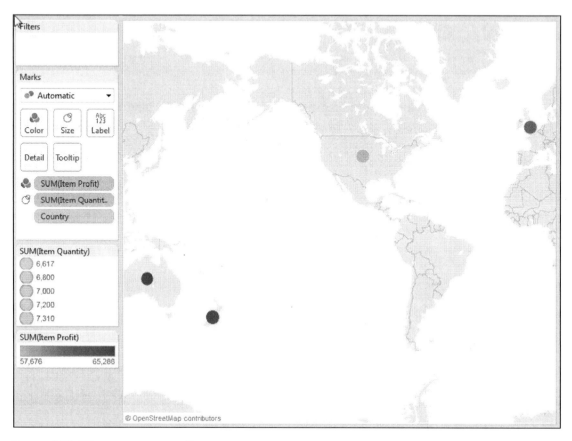

FIGURE 149: WORKED EXAMPLE - CHANGING SIZE AND COLOR

We will increase the variance in size of the circles to make it easier to spot the largest volumes. Click on the top right hand corner of the size legend, and select "Edit Sizes"

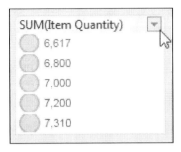

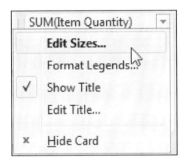

FIGURE 150: WORKED EXAMPLE - EDITING VARIANCE SIZE

We'll vary the sizes by range.

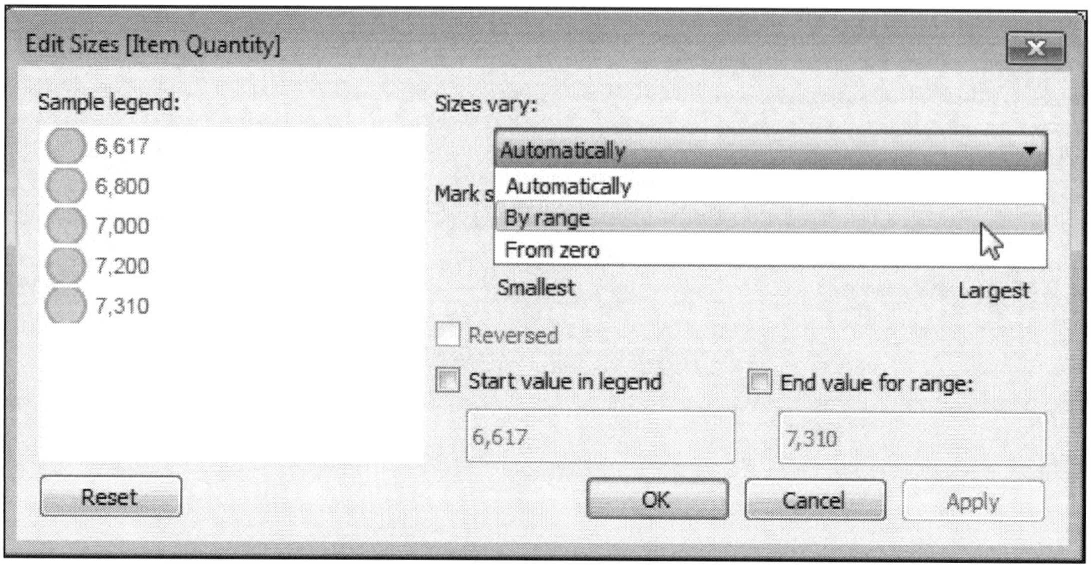

FIGURE 151: WORKED EXAMPLE - VARYING SIZE BY RANGE

Now adjust the mark size range to show a greater variation between the two ends of our size spectrum.

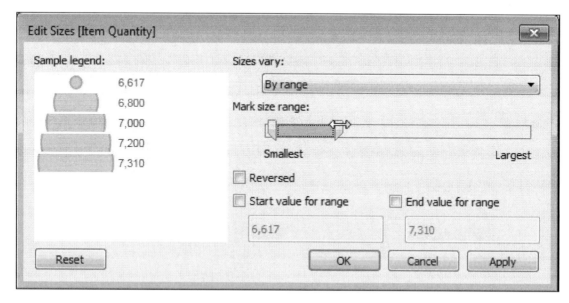

FIGURE 152: WORKED EXAMPLE - ADJUSTING MARK SIZE RANGE

Click OK and see the updated map to view your changes.

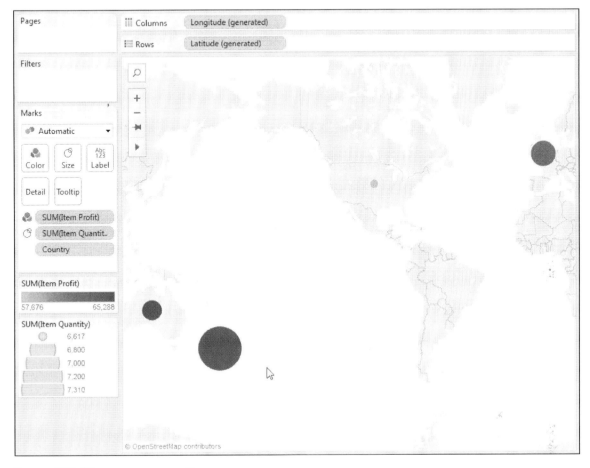

FIGURE 153: WORKED EXAMPLE - VIEWING SIZE

We will now edit the colors used in the viz to show "green" for most profitable and "red" for least profitable. This process is similar to editing the sizes. Use the drop down menu in the top right hand corner of the color legend.

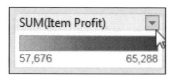

FIGURE 154: WORKED EXAMPLE - COLOR DROP DOWN MENU

Select "Edit Colors".

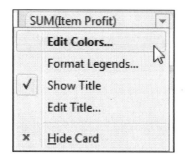

FIGURE 155: WORKED EXAMPLE - "EDIT COLORS"

Select your preferred color palette. For this example, we'll use the Red-Green Diverging palette.

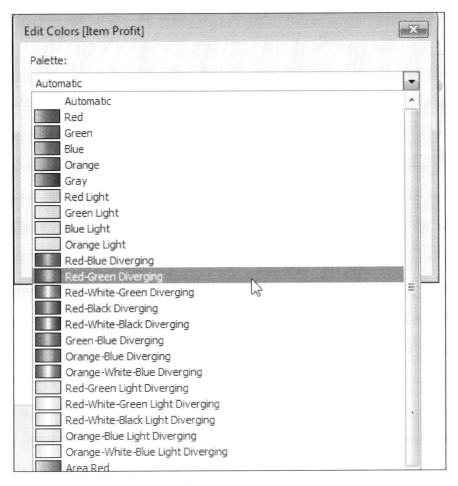

FIGURE 156: WORKED EXAMPLE - SELECTING A COLOR PALETTE

Click OK and see your changes reflected on the map.

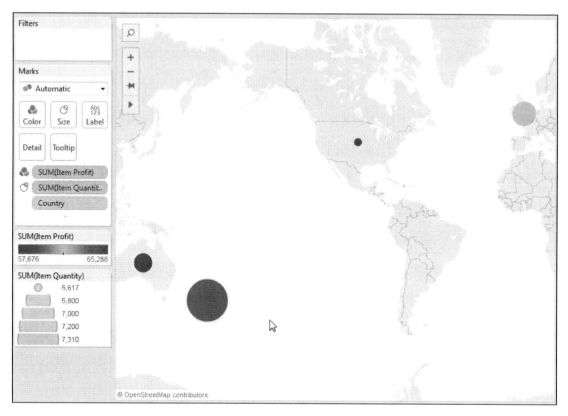

FIGURE 157: WORKED EXAMPLE - VIEWING COLOR CHANGES

You can see from the map now that the highest volume of sales comes from the New Zealand and Australian regions and that these regions are also more profitable than the United Kingdom and United States regions.

If Tableau does not recognize any geographic fields automatically, we can manually force Tableau to recognize geographic fields from a dimension of our choosing. For example, if you have a state or region field that Tableau has not recognized as a geographic field, simply right mouse click on that field and select "Geographic Role".

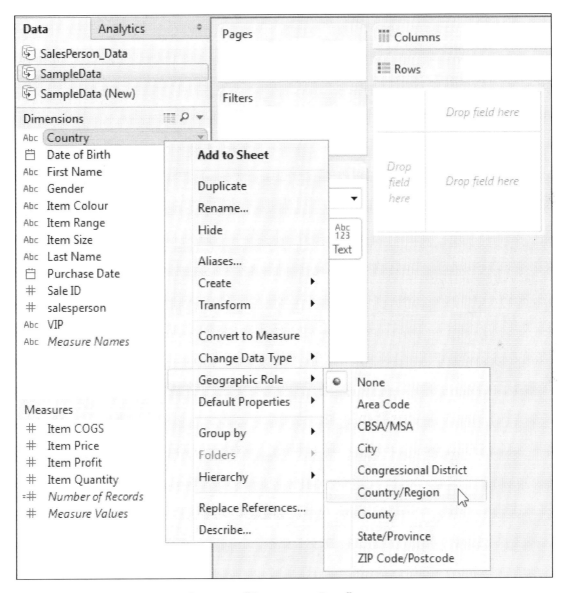

FIGURE 158: WORKED EXAMPLE - SELECTING "GEOGRAPHIC ROLE"

Select the geographic role that applies to that field. Now you have a field that is recognized as having a geographic role (as indicated by the globe icon) and can be used in building geographic maps.

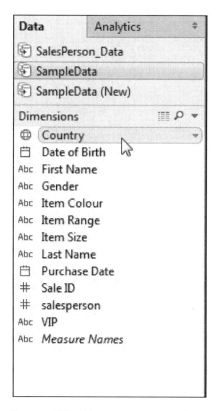

FIGURE 159: WORKED EXAMPLE - READY TO BUILD

3. SCATTER PLOTS

Scatter plots are a very helpful chart for visualizing the relationship between measures. They are also extremely useful when trying to quickly identify groupings or patterns in the data.

WORKED EXAMPLE: CREATING SCATTER PLOTS

For example, we may wish to identify a relationship between the Item Price and the quantity of sales. To do this, simply double click the Item Quantity and then the Item Price measures — the scatter plot will be drawn with a single mark representing the intersection of these measures.

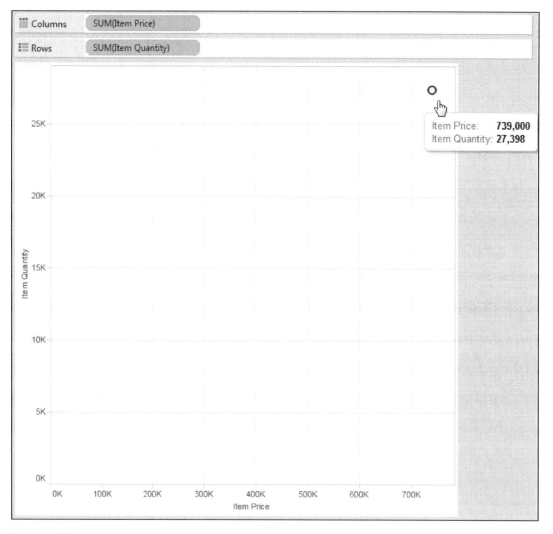

FIGURE 160: WORKED EXAMPLE - DRAWING A SCATTER PLOT

Note that each of the measures used has been placed on a separate column or row shelf, allowing the X and Y axis to be drawn.

To expand the scatter plot from one mark, place dimensions such as the Item Range to the detail section of the Marks Card.

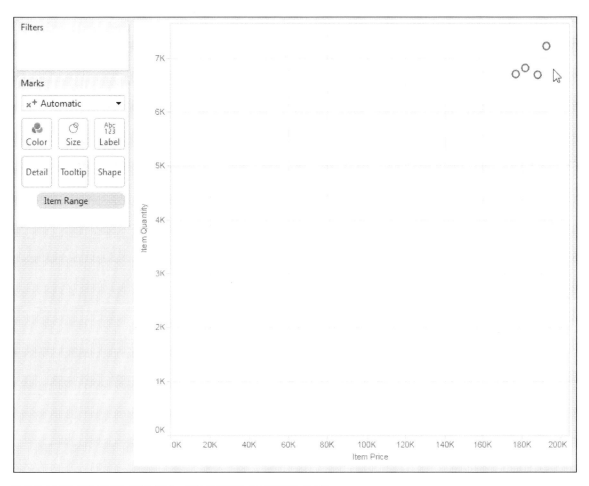

FIGURE 161: WORKED EXAMPLE - EXPANDING A SCATTER PLOT

Add dimensions to color, size and shape to give depth to your visualization.

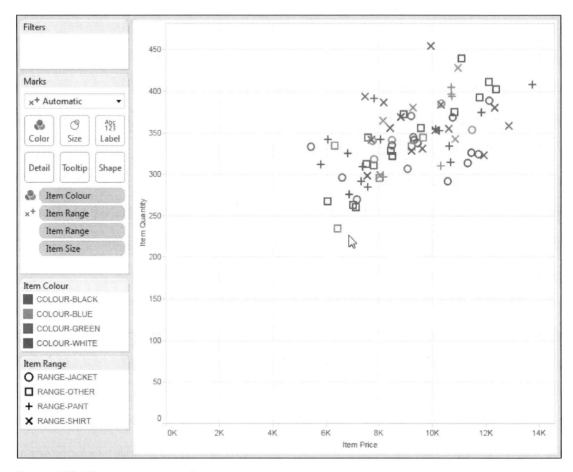

FIGURE 162: WORKED EXAMPLE - ADDING COLOR, SIZE, AND SHAPE TO A SCATTER PLOT

Using the same method described when building a geographic map, we can change the colors, sizes and shapes used in this viz by selecting the drop down menu from the appropriate legend.

Let's change the shapes used on the viz by selecting "Edit shape" from the drop down menu on the shapes legend.

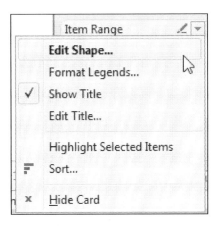

FIGURE 163: WORKED EXAMPLE - EDITING SCATTER PLOT SHAPE

There are a range of shape palettes to choose from — the possibilities are endless because you can also create custom shapes, which you learn how to create later in this book. For now, chose one of the existing shape palettes, such as "Filled".

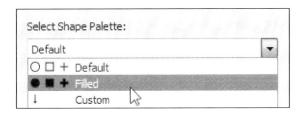

FIGURE 164: WORKED EXAMPLE - "FILLED" SHAPE PALETTE

You can assign specific shapes to specific data items by first selecting the data item and then selecting the particular shape.

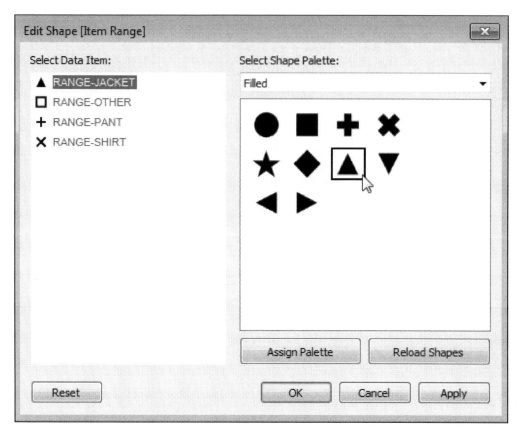

FIGURE 165: WORKED EXAMPLE - ASSIGNING SHAPES TO DATA ITEMS

Once you have made the necessary changes, click "Apply".

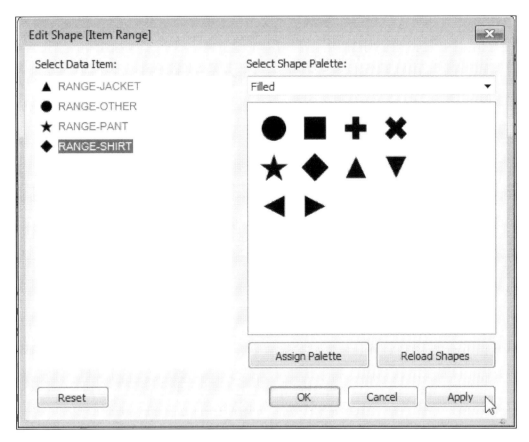

FIGURE 166: WORKED EXAMPLE - MAKING SHAPE CHANGES

Your scatter plot will now reflect each of the color, shape and size preferences you have set.

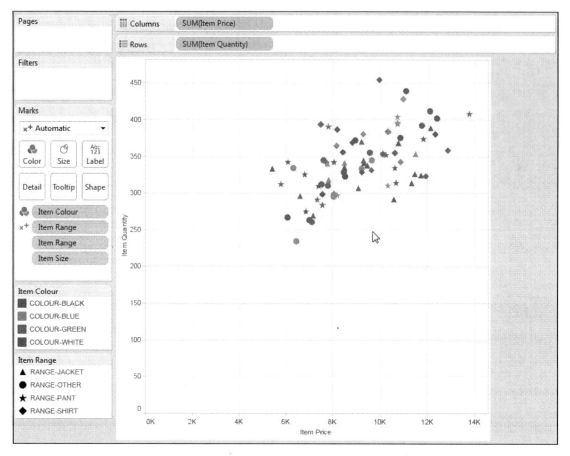

FIGURE 167: WORKED EXAMPLE - REFLECTING CHANGE

4. PIE CHARTS

There is much debate within the data-viz community as to whether or not pie charts should ever be used in data visualization (with the vast majority of vizers agreeing pie charts should never be used!). Pie charts can be difficult to interpret — the human eye cannot easily judge angles and variations between slices of the pie, particularly when there are many slices. However, in many organizations, pie charts are part of the furniture! Pie charts are as common in organizational reporting as dirty cups in the dishwasher.

So if you must use pie charts, here's how to do it using Tableau.

WORKED EXAMPLE: CREATING PIE CHARTS

Firstly, we need a measure that we can divide up to be our pie! Double click on a measure or drag the measure to the rows shelf.

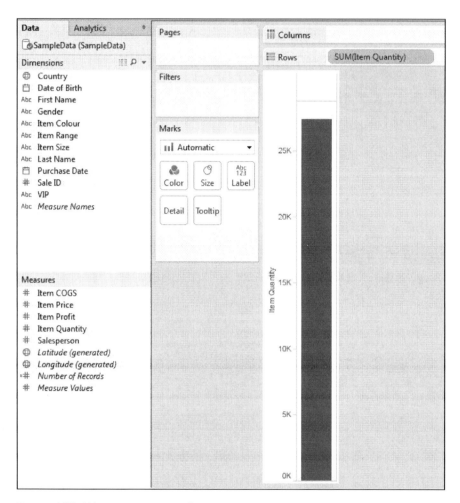

FIGURE 168: WORKED EXAMPLE - SELECTING A MEASURE FOR A PIE CHART

On the marks card, use the drop down to select "Pie Chart".

FIGURE 169: WORKED EXAMPLE - SELECTING "PIE CHART"

Drag the measure onto the detail card.

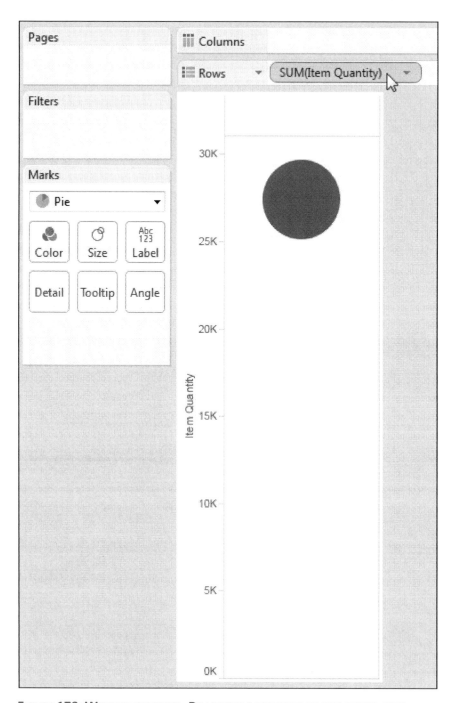

FIGURE 170: WORKED EXAMPLE - DRAGGING A MEASURE TO THE DETAIL CARD

To position the pie in the center of the viz and remove the "Item Quantity" Axis, drag the Item Quantity pill to the detail section of the Marks Card.

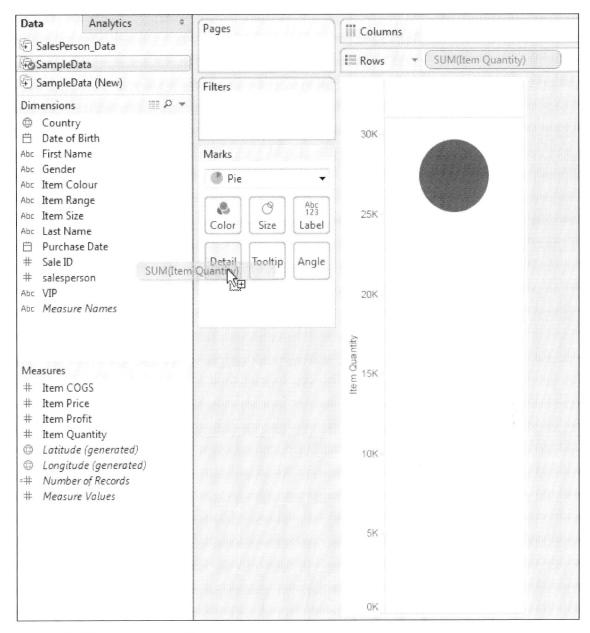

FIGURE 171: WORKED EXAMPLE - POSITIONING PIE CHARTS IN THE CENTER

To add slices to the pie, drag different dimensions onto the color card.

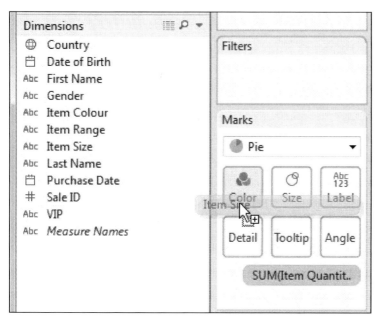

FIGURE 172: WORKED EXAMPLE - ADDING PIE SLICES

Your pie will be sliced according to categories available in that dimension.

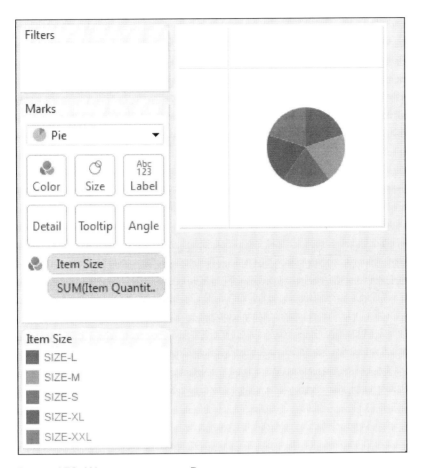

FIGURE 173: WORKED EXAMPLE - PIE SLICES

You can edit the colors of the pie by clicking on the color card.

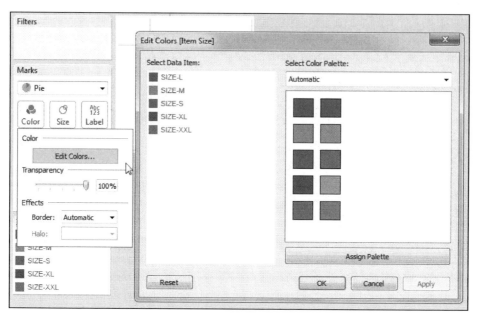

FIGURE 174: WORKED EXAMPLE - EDITING COLORS

You can add labels by dragging a measure to the label card.

FIGURE 175: WORKED EXAMPLE - ADDING LABELS TO A PIE CHART

And you can change the value displayed in the label by clicking on the options associated with that measure.

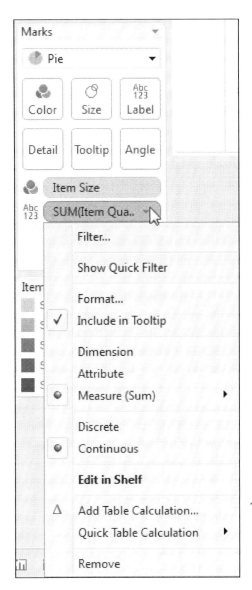

FIGURE 176: WORKED EXAMPLE -CHANGING VALUE DISPLAYED

For example, you might want the labels to show the percentage of the pie. Do this by clicking on "Quick Table Calculation" and selecting "Percent of Total".

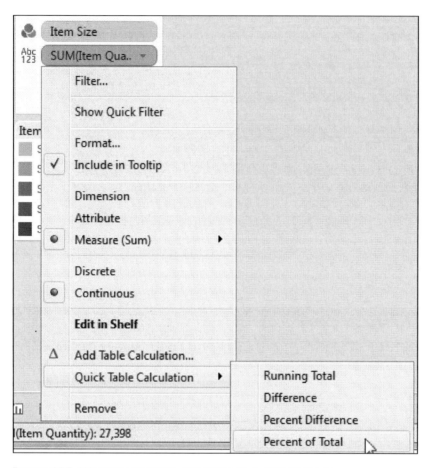

FIGURE 177: WORKED EXAMPLE - PERCENTAGE OF THE TOTAL LABELS

You can also add text labels to the pie chart to indicate what each color represents. Simply drag a dimension to the label card and the label will be displayed on the pie chart.

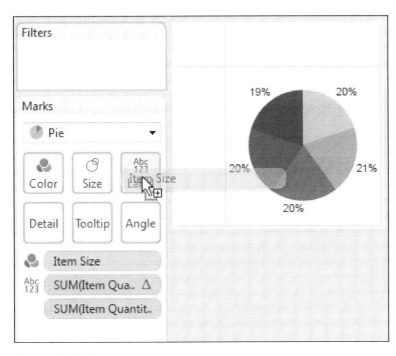

FIGURE 178: WORKED EXAMPLE - ADDING TEXT LABELS

5. DUAL AXIS CHARTS

An extremely common chart type in business circles is the dual axis chart. Whilst the name of this type of chart may appear daunting, you are probably more familiar with this type of chart than you realize!

This is a commonly used chart in the business community that displays two related measures. A common example of where a dual axis chart is used in business is to compare quantity of sales to the value of sales, or profitability of those sales.

WORKED EXAMPLE: CREATING DUAL AXIS CHARTS

Let's start by creating a simple bar chart to show the quantity of sales over a time series. First, drag Purchase Date to the Columns shelf and set this to Discrete.

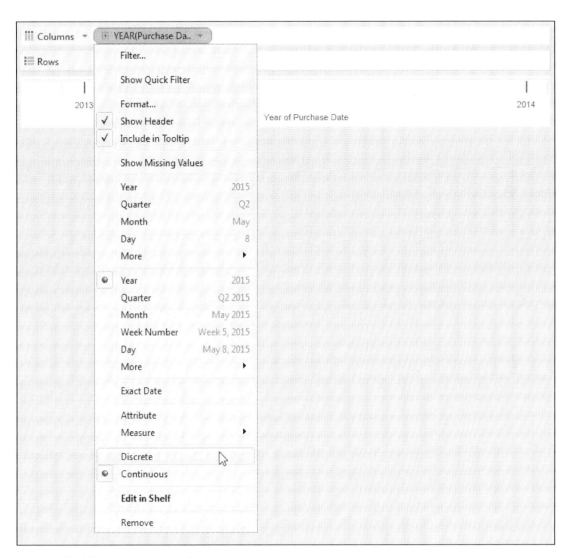

FIGURE 179: WORKED EXAMPLE - SET TO DISCRETE

Expand this date field to display 'Months' by clicking the + symbol on the blue pill.

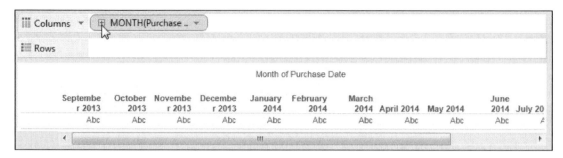

FIGURE 180: WORKED EXAMPLE - EXPANDING TO MONTHS

Now drag Item Quantity to the Rows shelf so that a line chart appears.

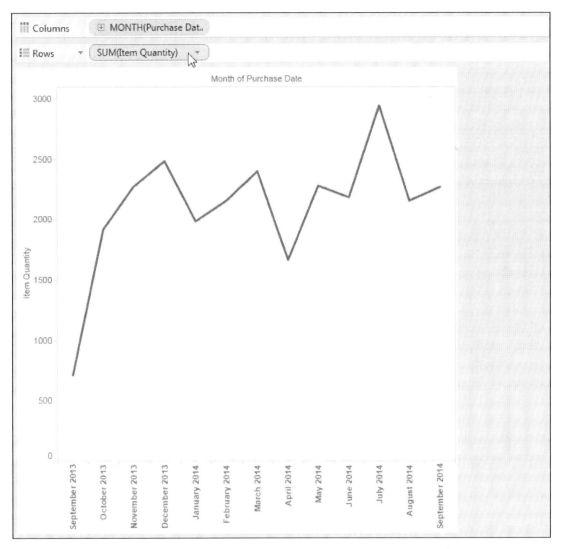

FIGURE 181: WORKED EXAMPLE - INITIAL LINE CHART

Go to the Marks Card and select "Bar" from the drop down menu.

FIGURE 182: WORKED EXAMPLE - SELECTING BAR

And we have the first half of our dual-axis chart.

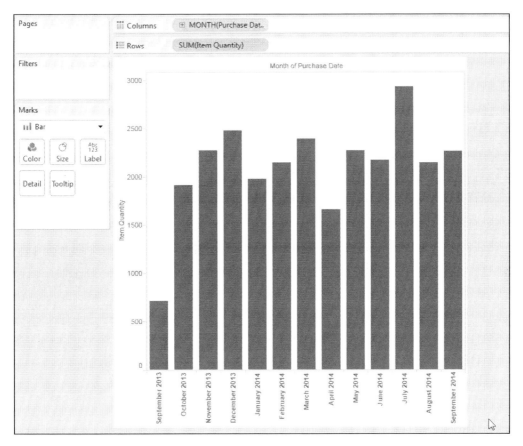

FIGURE 183: WORKED EXAMPLE -FIRST HALF OF DUAL-AXIS CHART

Dual axis refers to using a second axis on the one chart. The second axis can either be a second X axis or a second Y axis. In this example, we'll be creating a second Y axis to display the item profit for the same time series as the item quantity already in our viz.

Drag the Item Profit measure to the Rows shelf and place next to the Item Quantity pill.

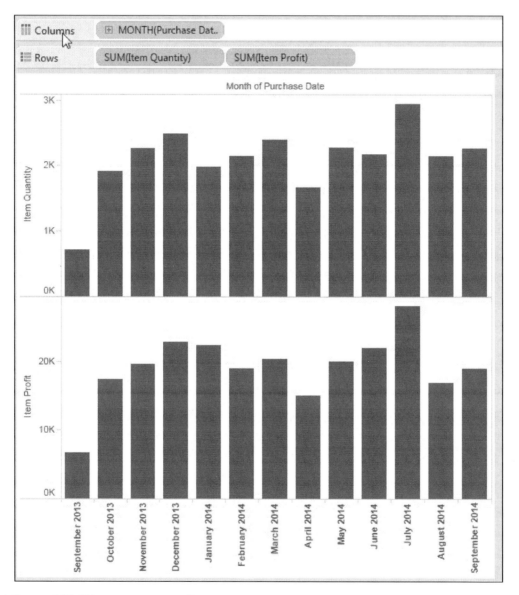

FIGURE 184: WORKED EXAMPLE - CREATING THE SECOND AXIS

Tableau has recognized that the two measures share the same time series, but it has plotted the two measures as separate charts.

Use the drop down menu on the Item Profit pill to select "Dual Axis".

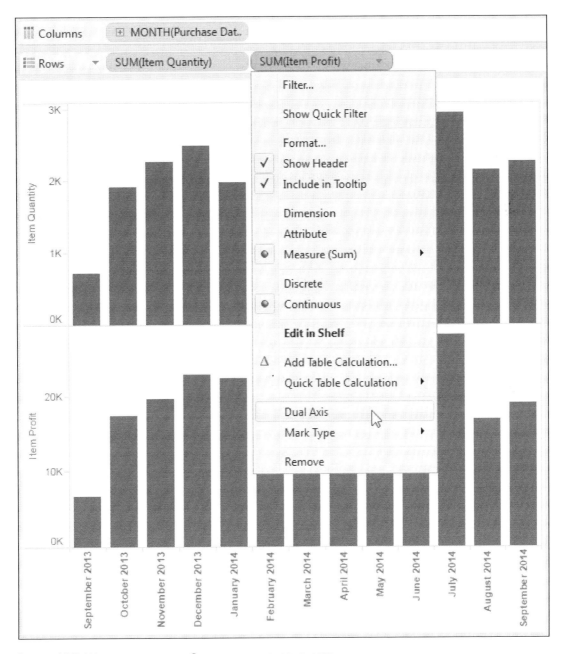

FIGURE 185: WORKED EXAMPLE - SELECTING THE SECOND AXIS

You will see that the two measures have effectively been placed on top of each other, with each measure being assigned a different color. Note also the two axes — or dual axes — that now frame the viz.

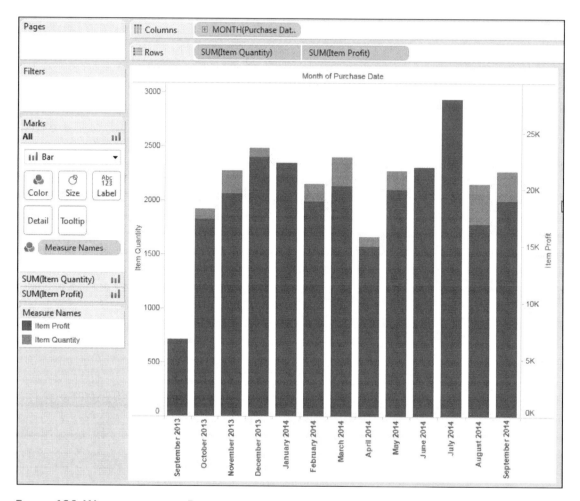

FIGURE 186: WORKED EXAMPLE - DUAL AXIS CHART

To change either of the measures to a line chart, simply click on the measure you wish to adjust on the Marks Card in order to expand the Marks Card options for only that particular measure. Clicking the Item Profit Marks Card will allow you to make changes to the Item Profit marks only (i.e. – not the Item Quantity marks)

FIGURE 187: WORKED EXAMPLE - CHANGING MEASURES

Use the drop down menu to select "Line".

FIGURE 188: WORKED EXAMPLE - CHANGING TO "LINE"

The dual axis chart will update accordingly.

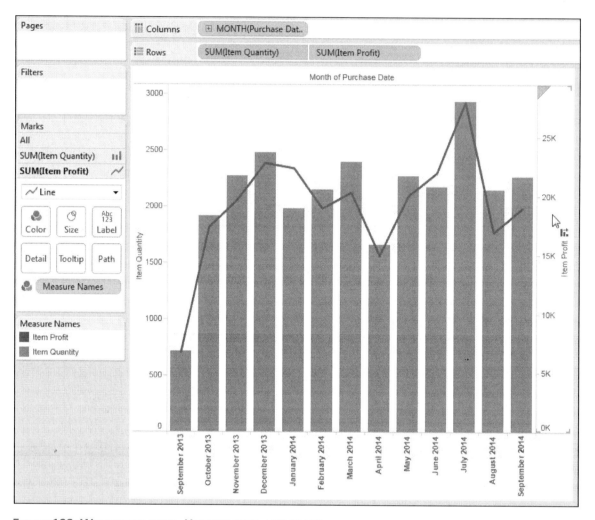

FIGURE 189: WORKED EXAMPLE - UPDATED DUAL AXIS CHART

By clicking "All" on the Marks Card, we can edit the settings for all marks on the viz (i.e. both the Item Quantity and the Item Profit marks).

FIGURE 190: WORKED EXAMPLE - EDITING THE SETTINGS FOR MARKS

Notice a new pill called Measure Names has been used to define color on the Marks Card?

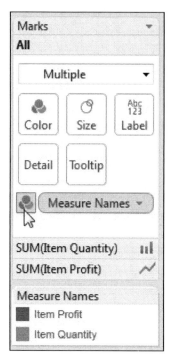

FIGURE 191: WORKED EXAMPLE - MEASURE NAMES

If we click "Color" and then select "Edit Colors", we can edit the colors for both Item Quantity and Item Profit at the same time.

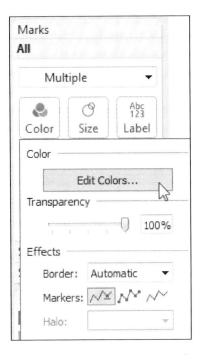

FIGURE 192: WORKED EXAMPLE - EDITING COLORS

Let's change Item Quantity to light grey and Item Profit to red so it stands out.

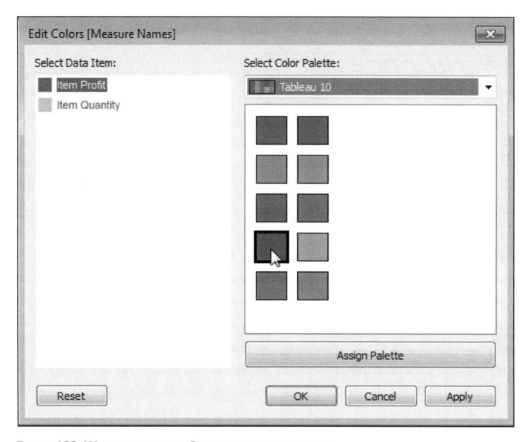

FIGURE 193: WORKED EXAMPLE - CHANGING TO GREY AND RED

Click OK and view the resultant viz.

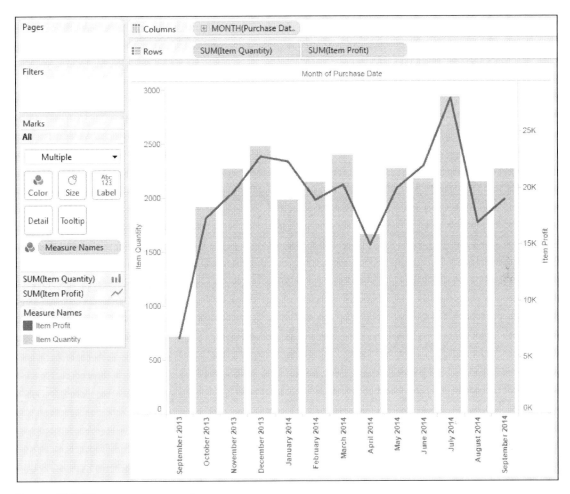

FIGURE 194: WORKED EXAMPLE - ADJUSTED DUAL AXIS GRAPH

As demonstrated in earlier sections, we can change the format of either axis by simply right-mouse clicking the axis and making relevant changes. To change the format of the date displayed, right-mouse click on the date and select "Format".

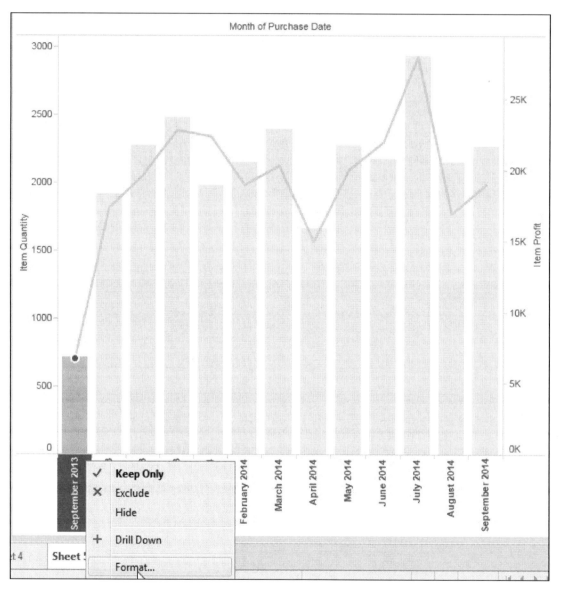

FIGURE 195: WORKED EXAMPLE - SELECT "FORMAT"

The formatting tools will appear on the left of the screen. Use the drop down menu to select from the range of formats available for dates.

FIGURE 196: WORKED EXAMPLE - FORMATTING TOOLS

If you cannot find a format you wish to use, you can use a custom date format using the following formats:

d	Display the day as a number without a leading zero (1 31).
dd	Display the day as a number with a leading zero (01 31).
ddd	Display the day as an abbreviation (Sun Sat).
dddd	Display the day as a full name (Sunday Saturday).
ww	Display the week of the year as a number (1 54).
m	Display the month as a number without a leading zero (1 12).
mm	Display the month as a number with a leading zero (01 12).
mmm	Display the month as an abbreviation (Jan Dec).
mmmm	Display the month as a full month name (January December).
q	Display the quarter of the year as a number (1 4).
yy	Display the year as a 2-digit number (00 99).
yyyy	Display the year as a 4-digit number (100 9999).

Meaning mm-yy would appear as 10-15 for October 2015 and dd/mmmm/yyyy would appear as 19/October/2015.

Enter the custom date format you wish to use.

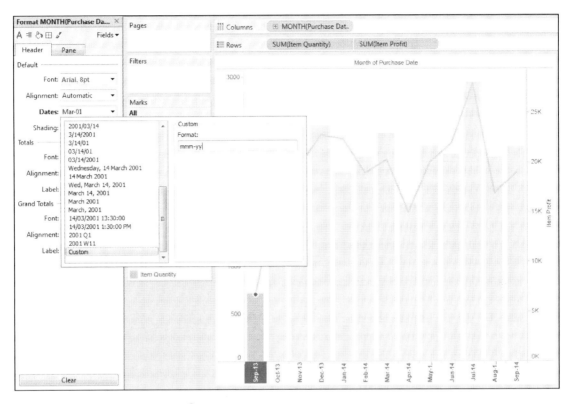

FIGURE 197: WORKED EXAMPLE - CREATING A CUSTOM DATE

To rotate the date labels so they can more easily be read, right-mouse click the date and select "Rotate Label".

FIGURE 198: WORKED EXAMPLE - SELECT "ROTATE LABEL"

Now we have a nicely formatted dual-axis chart showing the quantity of items sold and the item profit for each calendar month.

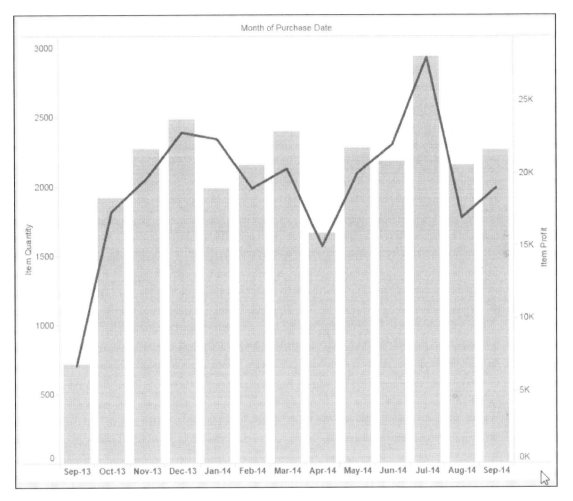

FIGURE 199: WORKED EXAMPLE - COMPLETED DUAL AXIS CHART

6. CROSSTABS AND TABLES

I'm a firm believer in tailoring information to suit the audience. I think it's important to cater for all types of preferences for reading and understanding data. Some of your stakeholders may be more visually inclined than others, or they may respond well to charts and other visualizations. However, there may also be some stakeholders who prefer hard and fast numbers, detailed tables and raw values.

The challenge lies in finding the right balance between these stakeholders and catering to their needs in a way that invites them to explore the dashboard and visualization, and to look past the format and instead look to the insights within the data.

There's a reason why I left this data visualization staple to the end. Tableau is a data visualization tool — it creates beautiful visualizations and engaging data interactions. That's not to say it can't also do crosstabs and tables. In fact, Tableau does tables very well (and very quickly!)

I often like to use both visualization and a corresponding table of values on dashboards I prepare for various audiences. The benefit of this it that all data-consumption preferences are catered for and, with a little Tableau magic, we can create a filter or highlight action to make the table responsive to any interaction with the visualization.

WORKED EXAMPLE: CREATING CROSSTABS OR TABLES

It's pretty easy to build tables by dragging and dropping pills on shelves and playing around with the results. However, Tableau's got a fantastic little feature that creates instant tables that match your visualization precisely! All you need to do is build your visualization. Right mouse click on the worksheet name where the viz lives and select "Duplicate as Crosstab".

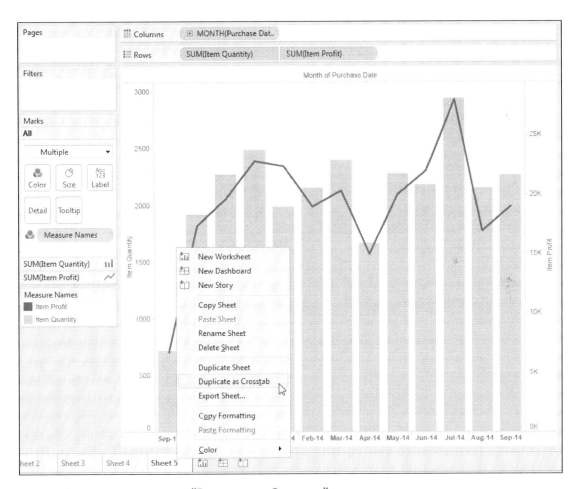

FIGURE 200: WORKED EXAMPLE - "DUPLICATE AS CROSSTAB"

Hey presto — instant table!

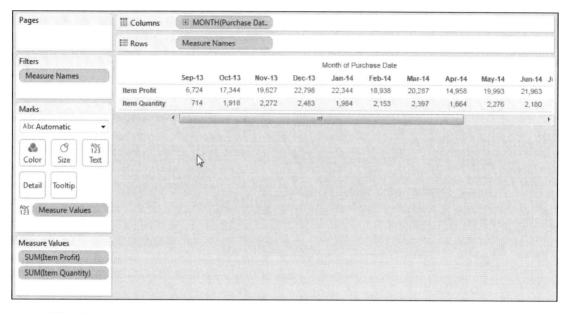

FIGURE 201: WORKED EXAMPLE - INSTANT TABLE!

Try it for yourself on a couple of your vizes — it's a great way to quickly build a basic table that can be tweaked with different dimensions and measures as required, and so much faster than building a table or crosstab from scratch!

To add column or row totals and subtotals, go to "Analysis" in the toolbar and select "Totals".

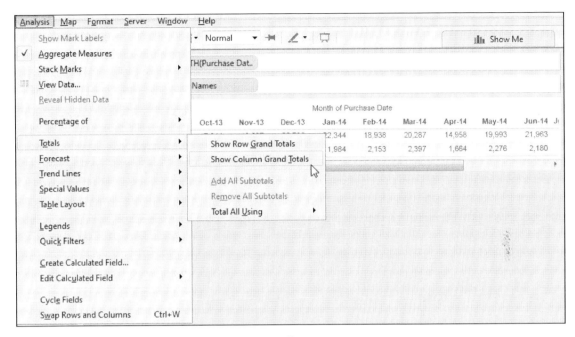

FIGURE 202: WORKED EXAMPLE - SELECTING "TOTALS"

Select the totals you wish to add to your table. These will automatically be calculated and added to the table for you.

	Jan-14	Feb-14	Mar-14	Apr-14	May-14	Jun-14	Jul-14	Aug-14	Sep-14	Grand Total
Item Profit	22,344	18,938	20,287	14,958	19,993	21,963	27,967	16,909	18,969	248,820
Item Quantity	1,984	2,153	2,397	1,664	2,276	2,180	2,940	2,152	2,265	27,398

FIGURE 203: WORKED EXAMPLE - ADDING "TOTALS" TO THE TABLE

Tableau has a number of built in "table calculations" that can be added to your tables with just a few clicks. To add basic calculations to the table such as "percent of total", or "running sum", go to the Measure Values shelf. Then, click on the drop down menu associated with the measure you wish to perform the calculation on.

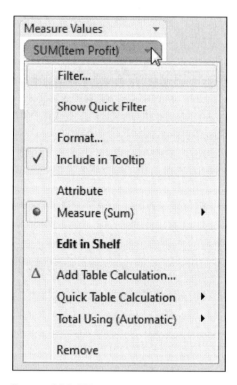

FIGURE 204: WORKED EXAMPLE - TABLE CALCULATIONS

In this example, we will calculate the running total of profit over the time series.

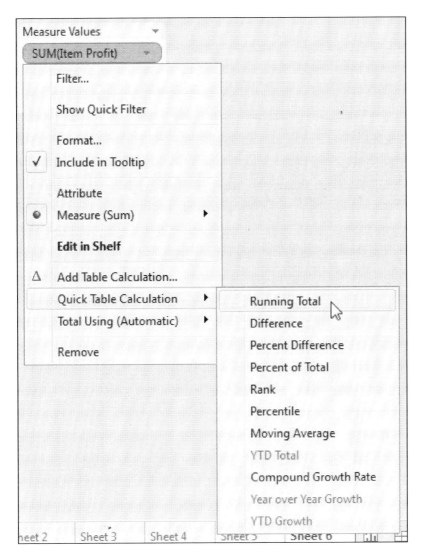

FIGURE 205: WORKED EXAMPLE - CALCULATING A RUNNING TOTAL

You'll notice the original Item Profit line in the table has been replaced with the running total of this measure — as identified by the triangle, or delta, inside the Item Profit pill.

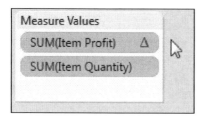

FIGURE 206: WORKED EXAMPLE - TRIANGLE/DELTA SYMBOL

You can add another instance of the Item Profit measure to the Measure Values card by simply dragging and dropping the Item Profit measure onto the card and releasing once you see the new pill in the required position.

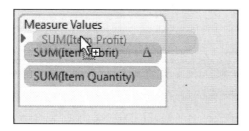

FIGURE 207: WORKED EXAMPLE - DRAGGING AND DROPPING MEASURES

Now you can see that the table has 3 rows: the top being item profit, the second being the running sum of item profit and finally, the item quantity.

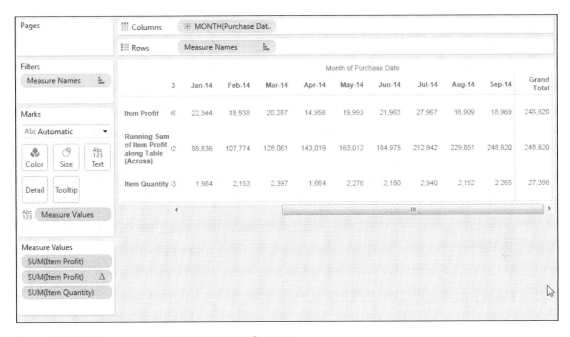

FIGURE 208: WORKED EXAMPLE - TABLE WITH 3 ROWS

7. USING FILTERS AND ACTIONS

When we build worksheets, we have the option to filter the data within that particular viz. However, we can also turn these filters into "quick filters" which can then be used by our stakeholders through controls on our dashboards. Different data types carry different filter options. Each of these filter options are explored below:

WORKED EXAMPLE: USING FILTERS

Strings

For string based dimensions, the filter dialogue box will present a list of the attributes within the dimension. You can select one, many or all of the individual attributes to add to your filter.

FIGURE 209: WORKED EXAMPLE – FILTERING BASED ON STRINGS

Discrete numbers (blue)

Similar to strings, the filter dialogue box for discrete numbers will present a list of numbers available within the field for you to select. You can select one, many or all of these options to add to your filter.

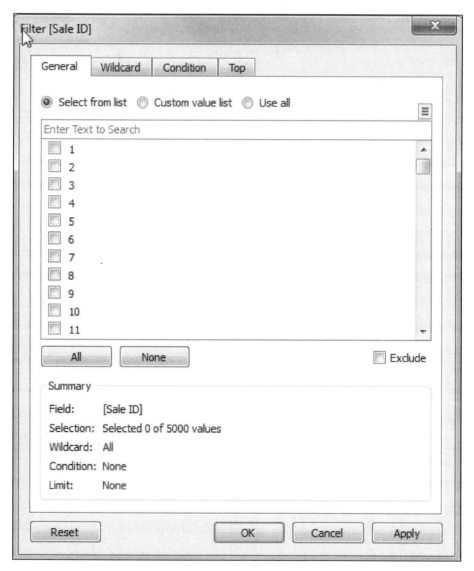

FIGURE 210: WORKED EXAMPLE - DISCRETE NUMBERS

Continuous numbers (green)

The filter dialogue box for continuous numbers is a little different. There are a number of ways filters can be applied to continuous numbers.

FIGURE 211: WORKED EXAMPLE - CONTINUOUS NUMBERS

By selecting "All values" and clicking "Next >", you'll be presented with a further dialogue box that allows you to set the filters for this field.

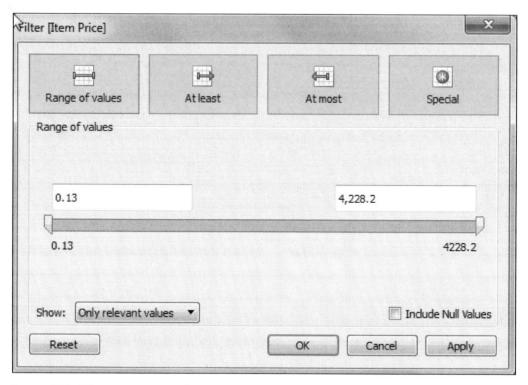

FIGURE 212: WORKED EXAMPLE - SETTING FILTERS USING CONTINUOUS NUMBERS

Here you can set minimums, maximums or ranges that the values within this field must meet in order to be included in the viz.

Going back to the previous step, if you select any of the other options (i.e. the mathematical functions listed) from this first dialogue box, that function will be applied to the data prior to the filter being applied.

FIGURE 213: WORKED EXAMPLE - MATHEMATICAL FUNCTIONS

For example, if we select "Average", our next dialogue box will present us with the filtering options to be applied to the average of our number — in this instance, the average item price.

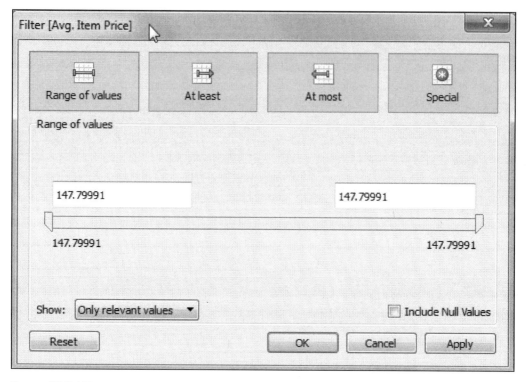

FIGURE 214: WORKED EXAMPLE – FILTERING BASED ON AVERAGES

Dates

Dates also have a number of ways in which they can be filtered.

The first dialogue box presents you with the following options:

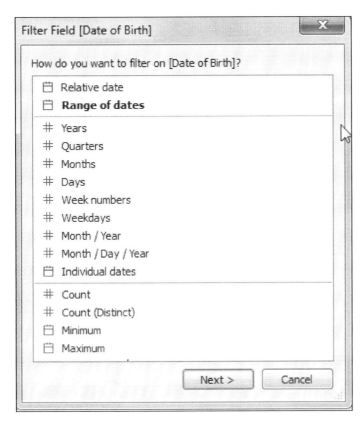

FIGURE 215: WORKED EXAMPLE – FILTERING DATES

Selecting either of the first two options will allow you to leverage the built-in date functions as outlined below:

Relative dates

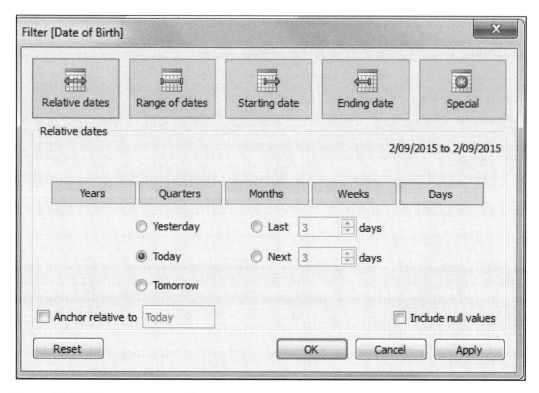

FIGURE 216: WORKED EXAMPLE - DATE FUNCTIONS

This filter option is handy if you want to show the current, last or next period of time such as last week, the last three months, last year, this month, etc.

Range of dates, Starting and Ending dates

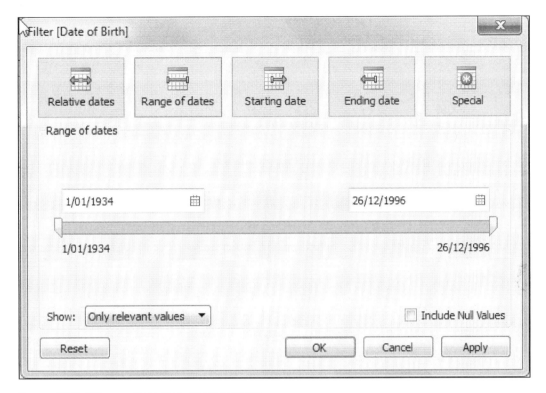

FIGURE 217: WORKED EXAMPLE - DATE RANGES

These options are useful if you have a specific date range that needs to be examined, such as a specific sales period or a promotional campaign.

To create a filter within a worksheet, drag and drop the dimension or measure you wish to filter on to the filters card.

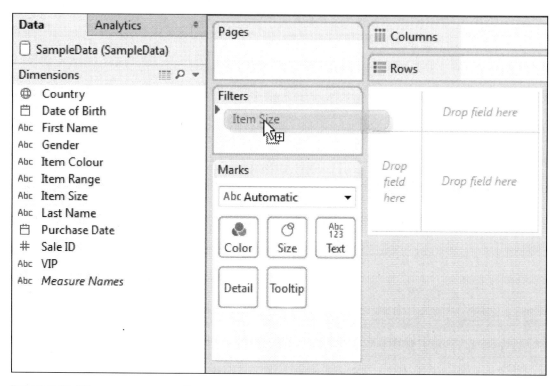

FIGURE 218: WORKED EXAMPLE - CREATING A FILTER

Once you have selected the required filter conditions, click OK and you will see the relevant pill now sitting within the filters card.

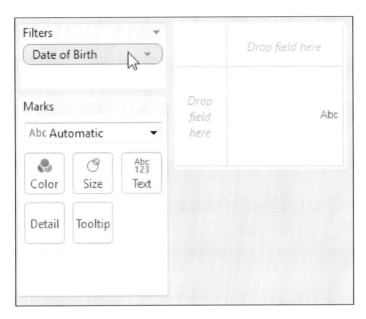

FIGURE 219: WORKED EXAMPLE -FILTER CONDITIONS

You will see that data on your worksheet has been filtered according to the conditions you have specified. Now we need to make these filters available for our stakeholders!

One way to do this is to right mouse click on the filter and select "Show Quick Filter".

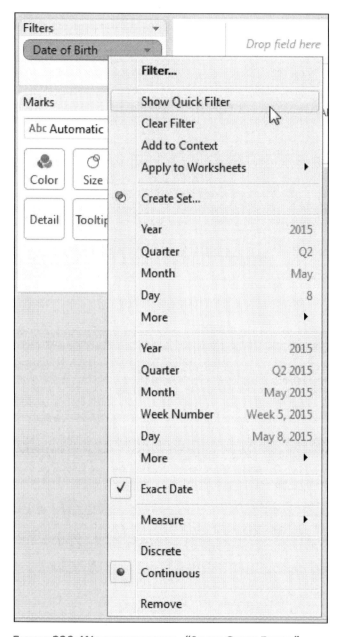

FIGURE 220: WORKED EXAMPLE - "SHOW QUICK FILTER"

This will create an interactive filter on the right of the screen that can now be used to filter the data.

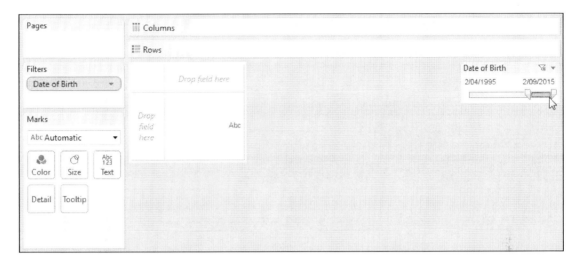

FIGURE 221: WORKED EXAMPLE - INTERACTIVE FILTER

When a worksheet with a visible quick filter is used in a dashboard, the associated quick filters are also made available for the dashboard.

DASHBOARDS

1. BUILDING WOW-WORTHY DASHBOARDS

In the previous sections we discussed sharing our work as being one of the important features of working with data. There is no point creating analysis and covering insights if we can't share them with people. Tableau allows us to create an enticing environment for people to interact with our data. For me, the real excitement in working with Tableau Desktop comes from the weaving of individual pieces together to create an awesome story and data exploration adventure for my stakeholders.

Once you've tackled the individual components that make up a dashboard — the worksheets — it's time to start building wow-worthy dashboards that will skyrocket you into data viz wonderland!

2. BASIC DASHBOARD COMPONENTS

Let's start thinking about our stakeholders again. If we understand well our stakeholders' needs of the dashboard, then we are going to deliver a better outcome for them.

Some of the basic components of any dashboard include:

- the right visualization, whatever sort of chart that might be,
- a table representing some of the key values in that visualization,
- relevant headline measures, and also
- a range of filters for the user to interact with.

When designing a dashboard, it is imperative to remember each component that we add to the dashboard is going to add to the complexity and also the performance of that dashboard. With this in mind, I like to keep the number of elements on the dashboard to four or less. This does not include the number of filters and parameters that you might use on the dashboard; rather it refers more to the number of charts, tables and other items such as headline measures.

WORKED EXAMPLE: CREATING A BASIC DASHBOARD

To create a dashboard in Tableau software, all we need to do is drag and drop our individual worksheets from our list of worksheets onto a new dashboard. To start a new dashboard, click on the dashboards tab and drag the worksheets that you have built into a layout that you desire on the dashboard.

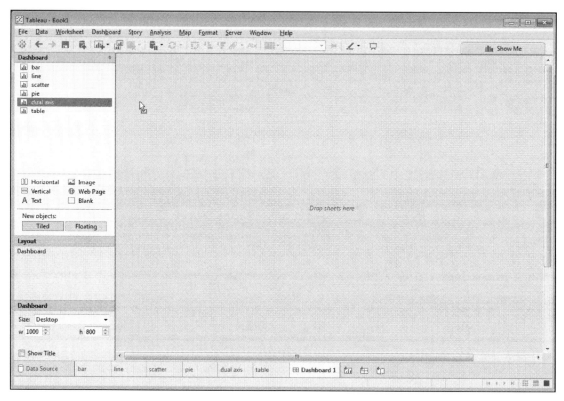

FIGURE 222: WORKED EXAMPLE - STARTING A NEW DASHBOARD

Pay careful attention when you are dragging and dropping items onto the dashboard. The greyed out area is in the location that you wish the worksheet to appear.

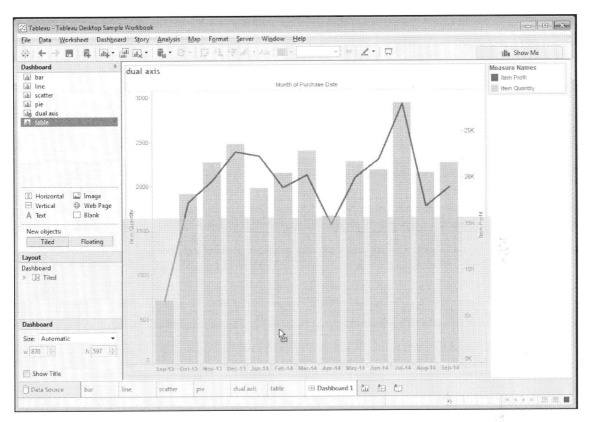

FIGURE 223: WORKED EXAMPLE - WORKSHEET AREA

When I talk about building dashboards, I often think about of the dashboard as a Tetris map: we can move blocks on top of each other, beside each other, underneath each other or over the top of each other in order to create our map.

For example, if I wanted a set of headline measures to run across the top of the dashboard and I already had one worksheet on the dashboard, I would hover my headline measures worksheet towards the top of the dashboard until I see a grey shaded area.

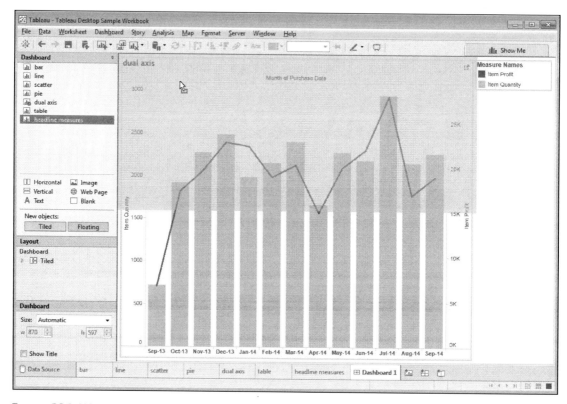

FIGURE 224: WORKED EXAMPLE - ADDING HEADLINE MEASURE TO DASHBOARD

This indicates that when I release my headline measure worksheet, it will drop into this position.

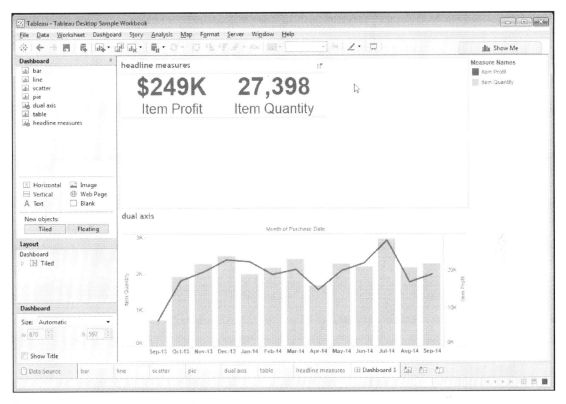

FIGURE 225: WORKED EXAMPLE - HEADLINE MEASURE POSITIONED

Once you have all elements or worksheets that you wish to include positioned on the dashboard, now is the time to start thinking about the formatting of that dashboard.

WORKED EXAMPLE: FORMATTING DASHBOARDS

The first thing I like to do when formatting a dashboard is to fix the size of the dashboard. This means that when this dashboard is rendered or displayed in whatever method you are using to share the dashboards, it will always render correctly, i.e. it will always look the way you wanted it to look. To do this, click on white space inside the dashboard. You will see dashboard sizing filters appear in the bottom left hand corner. From here you can select the size of the dashboard.

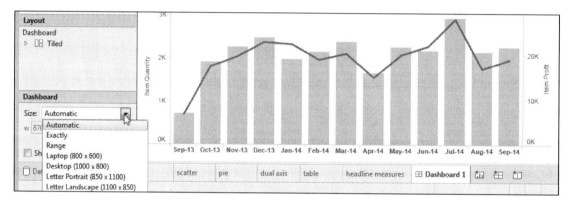

FIGURE 226: WORKED EXAMPLE - DASHBOARD SIZING OPTIONS

Again, this comes back to your stakeholder requirements. If your stakeholders like using iPads and other mobile devices such as Android tablets, it may be worthwhile setting the size of the dashboard to this resolution. This means your dashboards will always appear perfectly on those devices. I like to call this "building for the lowest common denominator".

For example, if I fix a dashboard size to iPad landscape, this will fit perfectly whenever accessed on an iPad device. If this is accessed on a desktop device, the dashboard will position itself in the center of the screen and divide white space around the edges. By fixing the size of the dashboard to the lowest common denominator (i.e. the smallest size or format my stakeholders are likely to use) I don't risk any misalignment or weird rendering — the dashboard will always look good on an iPad, but it will also render properly by centering itself on devices with larger display areas.

Next we need to get creative and make our dashboard as beautiful as it is functional. Take the time to resize elements, move legends, format filters and add instructional and narrative text as required.

To make vizes fill the space they are in, use the drop down menu at the top right hand corner of any viz element and select "Fit".

FIGURE 227: WORKED EXAMPLE - "FIT" OPTIONS

Selecting "Fit Width" will make the viz expand to fit the width of the pane it is in. "Fit Height" will expand the viz to fit the height of the pane it is in and "Entire View" will expand the viz to fit the entire pane.

Hide any unnecessary tiles, headings and field names by right mouse clicking on the offending text and selecting "Hide Title".

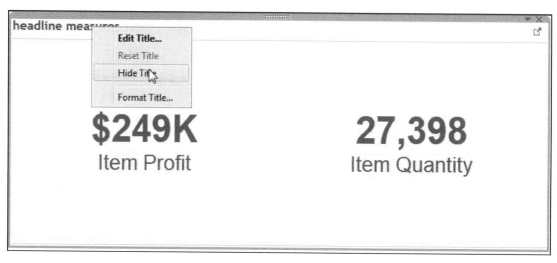

FIGURE 228: WORKED EXAMPLE - "HIDE" TITLE

Add text elements and blank elements to further customize your dashboard, and don't forget to add your company logo by dragging and dropping an image onto the dashboard and selecting the relevant image file!

FIGURE 229: WORKED EXAMPLE - CUSTOMIZING YOUR DASHBOARD

Once you have added the company logo as an image, right mouse click the top right hand corner of the image pane and select "Fit Image" — this will ensure the image will be displayed correctly no matter what space is available.

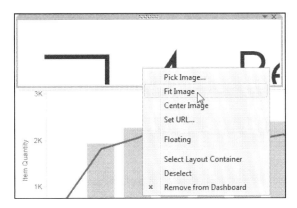

FIGURE 230: WORKED EXAMPLE - "FIT IMAGE"

Now you have a pretty smart looking dashboard!

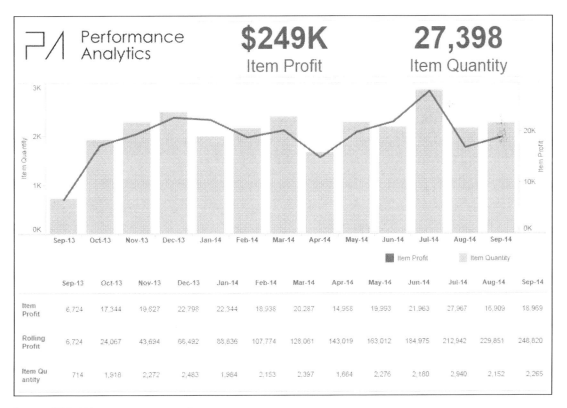

FIGURE 231: WORKED EXAMPLE - CUSTOMIZED DASHBOARD

3. HEADLINE MEASURES

Let's talk about headline measures. Headline measures form a critical part of any dashboard. I like to surface these in a very large font towards the top of the dashboard, so that when a user first logs in they can see these measures and they make sense to them. Think about news articles and television briefings — we are drawn in by the short, punchy headlines and we want to know more. Think of your headline measures as your news headlines. These are the measures that you want your stakeholders to be enticed by, so take time to choose the most interesting but also the most useful measures for your business.

Often when management or an executive looks to our dashboards, they are looking for short, sharp insights for areas of improvement or areas that are working well. If we want to create wow-worthy dashboards, we should look to surface some of the high level metrics or measures that our stakeholders are looking to know on a regular basis.

To this point, it is worth understanding firstly who your stakeholders are:

- who is looking to use this information?
- who will be referring to this information on a regular basis?
- what they are looking for in the information?

For example, are they after a daily update of stock levels? Are they after a comparison of sales volumes to previous years?

The better you can understand the stakeholder's needs, the more successful your dashboard will be.

4. FILTER ACROSS MULTIPLE ITEMS

Part of creating wow-worthy dashboards is about creating opportunities for our stakeholders to delve into the data in ways they may not have been able to before. The simplest way to do this is to build in filters which allow the user to slice and dice the data to their hearts' content, as discussed in the previous section on using filters and actions.

WORKED EXAMPLE: FILTERING ACROSS MULTIPLE ITEMS

Taking the worksheets created in previous worked examples, let's create an interactive experience for our stakeholders and allow them to filter by product range, product size and also region.

If we go back to our dual axis chart, we can add filters for item range, item size and country. Drag and drop these dimensions onto the Filters shelf. When the filter options for each dimension are presented, select "Use all".

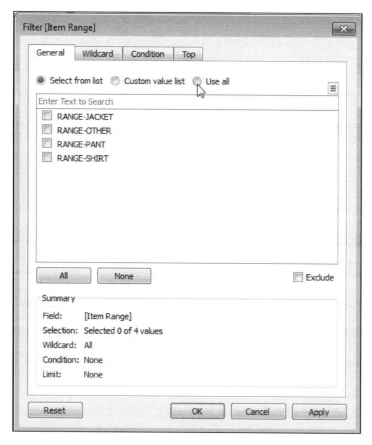

FIGURE 233: WORKED EXAMPLE - ITEM RANGE FILTERS

Once the "Use all" radio control has been selected and the list has been greyed out, click OK.

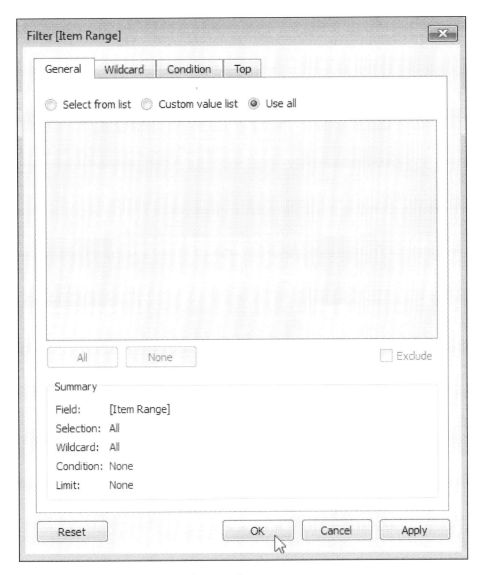

FIGURE 234: WORKED EXAMPLE - "USE ALL" RADIO CONTROL

Now that these filters have been created, go back to your dashboard and we'll use the dashboard functions to extend these filters to the relevant worksheets.

FIGURE 235: WORKED EXAMPLE – FILTERS SET AND READY TO GO

Use the drop down menu on the dual axis chart to locate the relevant quick filters.

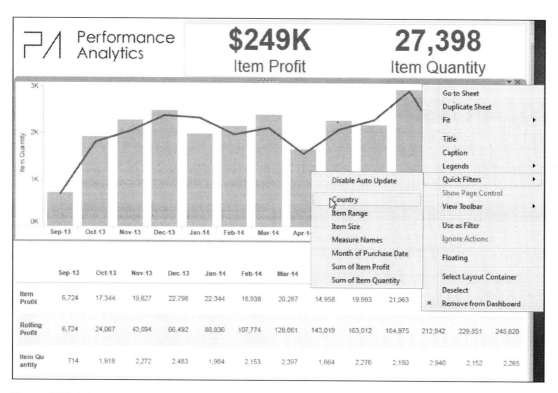

FIGURE 236: WORKED EXAMPLE - ACCESS QUICK FILTERS

Select each of the quick filters, one by one, and the filter options will appear on the right of the dashboard.

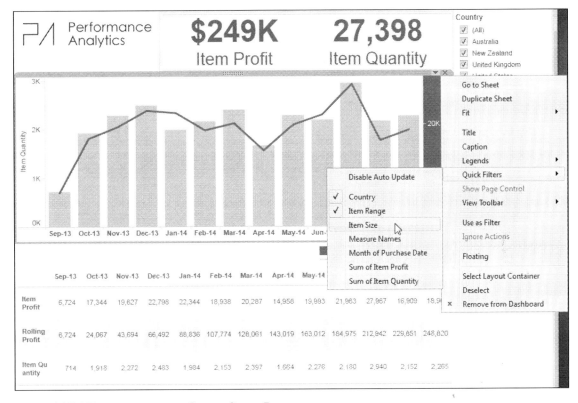

FIGURE 237: WORKED EXAMPLE – SELECT QUICK FILTERS

Once all of the filters have been made visible, we can use the filter controls by clicking the top right hand corner of each filter and setting each of these filters to apply to selected worksheets.

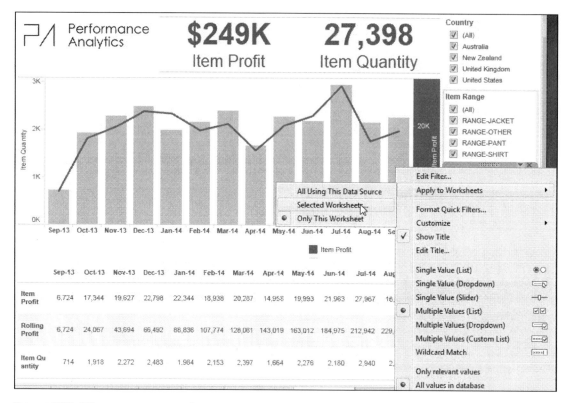

FIGURE 238: WORKED EXAMPLE – APPLY TO WORKSHEETS

Select "All on Dashboard" to set these filters to apply to each of the components of the dashboard and click OK.

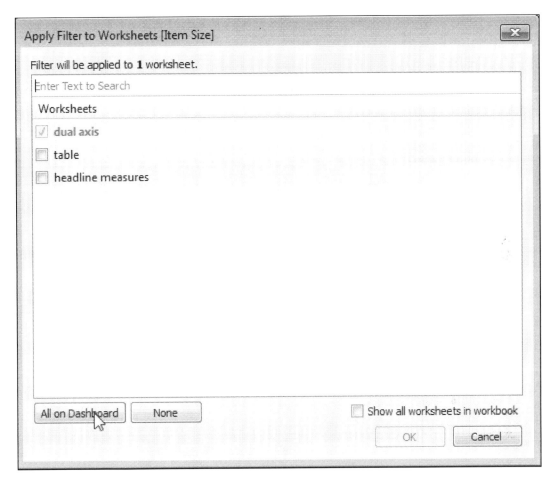

FIGURE 239: WORKED EXAMPLE - APPLYING FILTERS TO ALL WORKSHEETS ON DASHBOARD

Your filter will now control the results presented on each of the vizes, tables and headline measures contained on that dashboard.

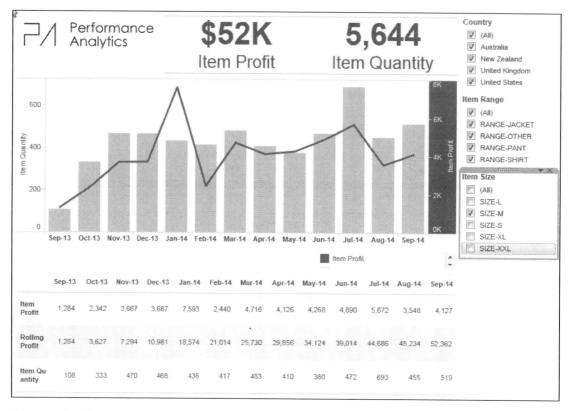

FIGURE 240: WORKED EXAMPLE – FILTERING ALL WORKSHEETS ON DASHBOARD

Again, using the filter controls found in the top right hand corner of each filter, select the most appropriate filter format.

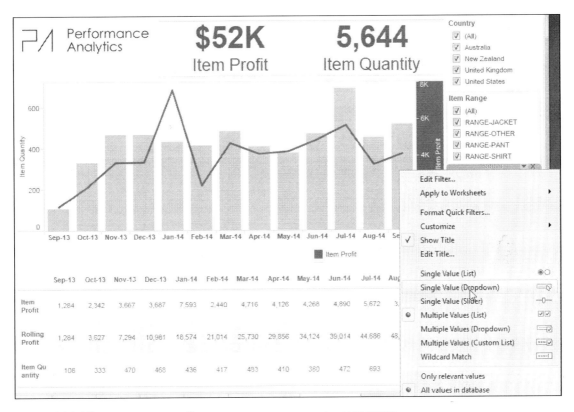

FIGURE 241: WORKED EXAMPLE - SELECTING THE MOST APPROPRIATE FILTER

Your dashboard is now complete with filters, headline measures, tables and charts, catering for all stakeholder preferences and looking pretty neat too!

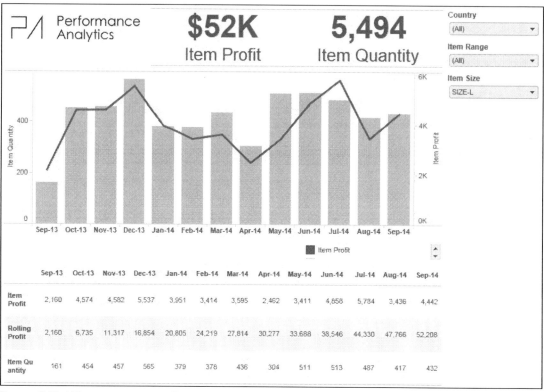

FIGURE 242: WORKED EXAMPLE - FINISHED DASHBOARD

5. INTERACTIVITY

Whilst filters provide a clean, structured mechanism to interact with dashboards created in Tableau Desktop, there are also a range of built in functions that allow the viz itself to function as a filter.

To use the dual axis chart to filter both the headline measures and the supporting table at the bottom of the dashboard, all you need to do is access the chart's controls at the top right hand corner of the viz and select 'Use as filter'.

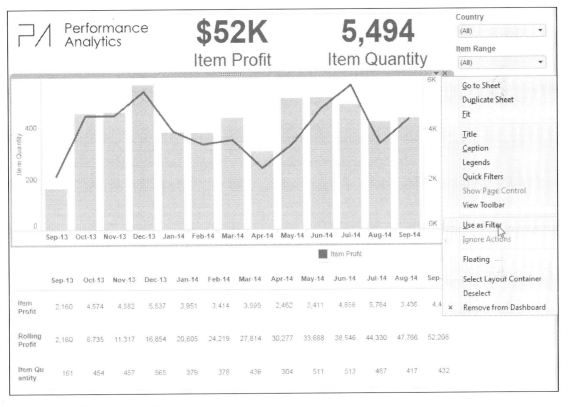

FIGURE 243: "USE AS FILTER"

Now if we click on a particular result on the viz, all other results will be filtered by that mark. For example, clicking the July 2014 Item Quantity updates the headline measures and the supporting table to show only the July 2014 results.

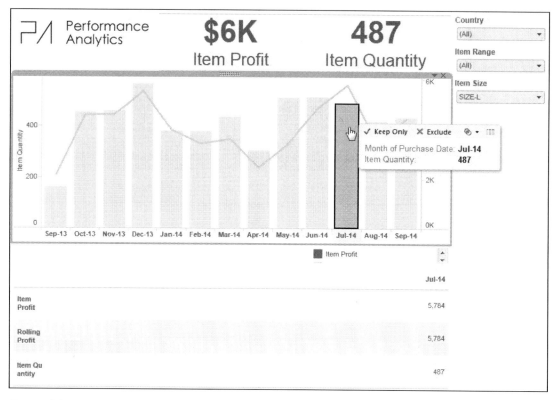

FIGURE 244: JULY 2014 RESULTS

Clicking the selected mark (the July 2014 bar) again will remove or undo the filter.

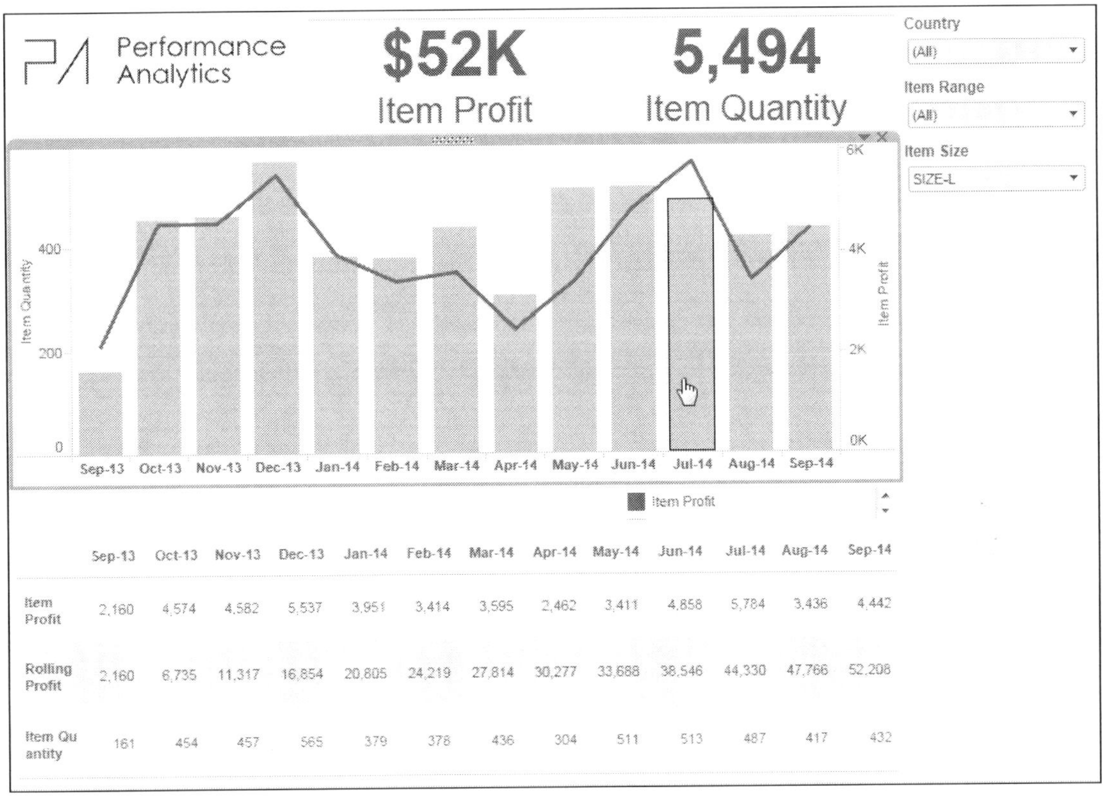

FIGURE 245: REMOVING A FILTER

Whilst this might not be the most helpful filter action in this dashboard, imagine examples where clicking the sales volume chart then updates a more detailed table showing individual sales volumes for particular item sizes, ranges, locations etc. Using a filter action in this sense provides the end user the ability to "drill down" and look at the underlying contributors to the aggregate totals.

6. FLOATING VS TILES

The final element of wow-worthy dashboards that we'll cover is the use of floating versus tiled objects.

On the dashboard controls pane, you'll notice the option for new objects to either be added as tiled or floating objects. Selecting either of these options prior to dragging and dropping a worksheet onto the dashboard determines how that object will be added to the dashboard.

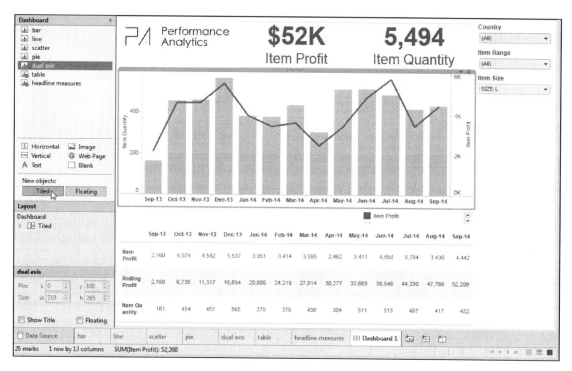

FIGURE 246: SELECTING TILED OBJECTS

I recommend always adding worksheet objects as tiled objects to the dashboard. This will give you a cleaner and more structured final result, with all elements following a grid like pattern which is pleasing to the eye and also more likely to render well on your stakeholders' screens and devices.

Objects can be changed from tiled to floating and vice versa once they are on the dashboard as well. This is particularly useful for small objects such as legends, instructional text, headings and company images that you may wish to float and maximize the space available on the dashboard.

To make an object float, go to the objects' controls at the top right hand corner of that object, and select "Floating".

FIGURE 247: MAKING AN OBJECT "FLOAT"

The object can then be moved to your desired location by dragging the item to its new home.

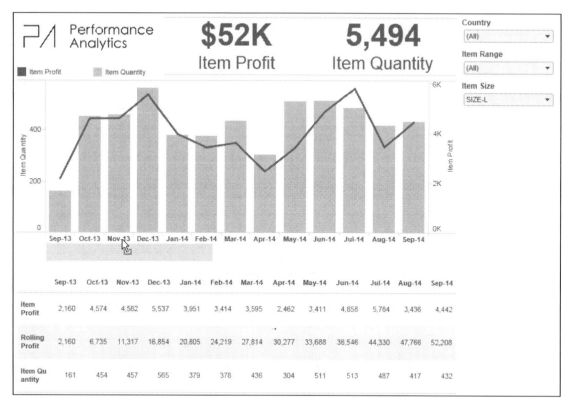

FIGURE 248: MOVING A FLOATING OBJECT

Using floating objects in this way allows you to make the most of every pixel of available space on your dashboard, as well as gives you the opportunity to locate related items closely together which can assist your audience when interpreting your visualizations.

DONE (TIME TO SHARE!)

Now that you have created your dashboards and visualizations, you'll definitely want to share these insights and discoveries. You will want to share your work with many internal, possibly even external, stakeholders to allow them to delight in the beauty and simplicity of your visualizations and to see for themselves the awesome interactivity and storytelling prowess you have unleashed!

This section is going to cover a range of ways that you can do that.

1. TABLEAU SERVER

Tableau Server is probably the most efficient way to share your dashboards and visualizations. Tableau Server allows you to organize your data sources to refresh automatically; it allows you to push and pull data between dashboards and visualizations, and it allows the security to be controlled by your internal IT security teams. Depending on security levels, your Tableau Server may or may not be accessible outside of your virtual or physical network environment. This may be a consideration for you when you are working out how to best share your visualizations.

Tableau Server allows for the dashboards and vizes to be accessed via an internet browser. All leading internet browsers are supported by Tableau Software. Users can interact with the dashboards and the visualizations if they have permission to do so and they can actually subscribe to dashboards and visualizations if that feature has been configured on your Tableau Server. Subscriptions will push a static view of the dashboard or visualization to the users' inbox on a schedule that they determine so they can stay up-to-date with the latest movements in data.

Consideration of the license costs for Tableau Server, the required configuration, management and administration, and, as mentioned earlier, whether or not Tableau Server is accessible outside the virtual or physical network may impede on whether you choose this option, particularly if you are dealing with external stakeholders.

Pros	Cons
Interactive experience for end users	Cost
Workbooks and data sources can be refreshed automatically	Administration and management of server and physical infrastructure required
Users can subscribe to views and workbooks	May be restricted by internal security
Up to date dashboards and data are accessible via internet browser, iPad or Android tablet	

2. TABLEAU ONLINE (TABLEAU SERVER 'IN THE CLOUD')

Tableau Online is a cloud-hosted version of Tableau Server that gives you all the benefits of Tableau Server outside your existing IT frameworks. Individual licenses can be purchased for around half the price of individual Tableau Server licenses; however, this is a recurring annual cost, as opposed to the once off license fee and then annual maintenance cost of Tableau Server licenses.

The Tableau Server used in Tableau Online is maintained by Tableau Software and therefore you have the benefit of Tableau Server being maintained and administrated by the experts in this field.

Tableau Online is a great way to share your vizes if you have a small number of users who need to be able to interact with the data and visualizations in a secure way. Tableau Online, being a cloud-hosted solution, allows for individuals inside and outside your business — wherever internet access exists — to be able to access the dashboards and visualizations either through an internet browser or through Tableau Software's iPad and Android apps.

Pros	Cons
Interactive experience for end users	Cost
Workbooks and data sources can be refreshed automatically	Administration and management of server environment required
Users can subscribe to views and workbooks	Data must be extracted and published to Tableau Online — live data connections are not possible
Dashboards and data are accessible via internet browser, iPad or Android tablet	
Physical infrastructure maintained and supported by Tableau Software	

3. TABLEAU PUBLIC

Tableau Public is basically a free version of Tableau Server — often used by data journalists and data viz enthusiasts to share their work and encourage public engagement with data visualizations. Being a free product, it is a very attractive option on face value; it provides anyone with an internet connection the ability to interact with dynamic and engaging dashboards and allows a growing community to share and critique each other's visualizations.

The main drawback to this is that there is no way to restrict the visualization or the data contained within to be accessed by the general public. Anything you publish to Tableau Public can be seen by the broader Tableau Public community. I caution any organization considering using Tableau Public to carefully think through the implications of their intellectual property and also their underlying data being exposed to an unrestricted audience.

Having said that, Tableau Public certainly does have some very good uses for business. Consider your annual report — you may wish to publish an interactive visualization of performance and embed that as part of your corporate website. You can do this, at no cost, by publishing your visualization on Tableau Public. If the information you are publishing is in the public domain, Tableau Public becomes a very useful and extremely cost effective (i.e. free!) tool for you to use.

My word of caution on using Tableau Public is that you should never put something on Tableau Public that you don't want the general public looking at, downloading and interacting with. Tableau Public is for sharing information that is in the public domain and information that you are happy to be shared with the world.

Pros	Cons
It's free!	Workbooks and associated data cannot be automatically refreshed — relies on publishing of packaged workbooks (including data extracts)
Accessible by anyone, anywhere	Accessible by anyone, anywhere
Physical infrastructure and server environment maintained and supported by Tableau Software	

4. TABLEAU READER

Creating packaged workbooks allow you to save the contents of your Tableau Desktop Workbook — including any extracted data that supports the visualizations you have created — and share this in much the same way as you would any other file with your colleagues. Another free product, Tableau Reader, allows your users to open and interact with the dashboards and visualizations that you have shared.

Tableau Reader is a good option for users who are looking to test the uptake and to try Tableau across the business before deciding which type of automated server environment is most appropriate for them.

A big drawback of this approach is that the workbook will not automatically update and refresh when your new data becomes available. So if your data is infrequently updated and of a relatively small file size, Tableau Reader may be a good solution for you in your business to share and interact with dashboards that have been developed. However, if your data is refreshed on a regular basis or needing to be refreshed on a regular basis, Tableau Reader will become more of a hindrance than a help in that packaged workbooks will need to be updated each time the data is refreshed in order for them to be up-to-date.

Pros	Cons
It's free!	Workbooks and associated data cannot be updated a new packaged workbook needs to be saved and shared if any changes or data refreshes are required
Receive a file like a PDF, but more interactive	Cannot be used on iPad or other mobile devices
No physical infrastructure or server environment maintenance required	The packaged workbook could be opened in Tableau Desktop which would allow full access to the data, worksheets and dashboards.

5. PRINT TO PDF

Finally, Tableau Desktop also has an option to Print to PDF, effectively creating a static visualization that can be shared as you would any other PDF.

The key drawback of this is that the interactive features you have included in your visualizations will not be available to the end users.

Pros	**Cons**
A quick and easy built-in feature of Tableau Desktop	Static output — no interaction available
Easily shared with multiple stakeholders. Users do not need any additional software	Workbooks and associated data cannot be updated a PDF needs to be saved and shared if any changes or data refreshes are required

Whilst these descriptions are intended to give you an overview of each of the options available to you for sharing your dashboards and visualizations, they are in no way, shape, or form a comprehensive overview of each of the products that have been named.

The comments provided here are intended to give you a brief overview only, and you should speak directly with Tableau Software if you require any additional information to support your decision as to whether to use Tableau Server, Tableau Public, Tableau Online or Tableau Reader.

THE FINISHING TOUCH

The following pages are what I would consider the 'optional extras'. These finishing touches are by no means a compulsory addition to your dashboards, but they do make a difference and can take a good dashboard to great!

1. REMOVING LINES / GRID LINES / OUTLINES

You may or may not have noticed, but each chart you build will be neatly framed by a pale grey border. This is due to the way Tableau thinks — in columns and rows — and these residual borders and outlines can be removed with a few simple clicks.

WORKED EXAMPLE: REMOVING LINES, GRIDLINES AND OUTLINES

Right mouse click inside the viz you wish to clean up and select "Format".

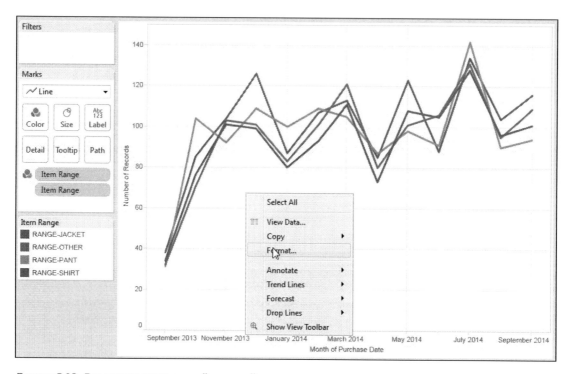

FIGURE 249: REMOVING LINES WITH "FORMAT"

This will launch the formatting controls in the left hand side of the screen.

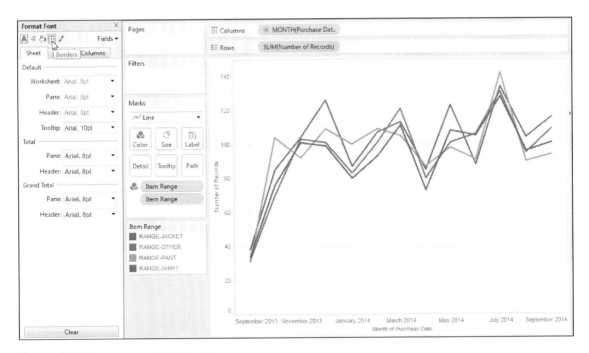

FIGURE 250: FORMATTING CONTROLS

Click the Borders icon (the one that looks like a window pane) and change each of the drop down menus to "None".

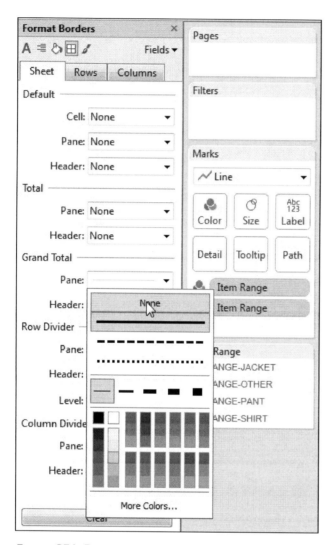

FIGURE 251: BORDERS ICON

This will remove the borders and outlines from the viz.

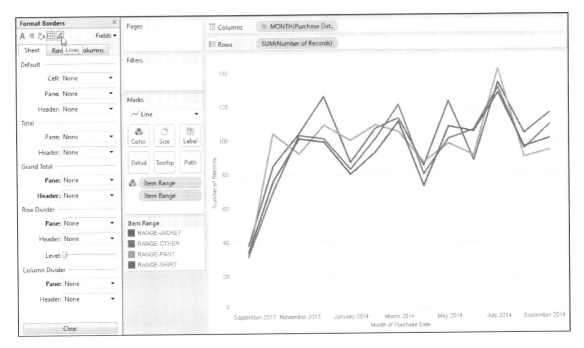

FIGURE 252: REMOVING BORDERS AND LINES

Click on the Lines icon (the one that looks like a paint brush) and use the drop down controls to remove gridlines and any other lines as required.

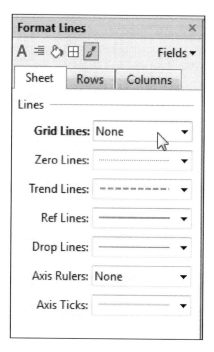

FIGURE 253: REMOVING BORDERS AND LINES

The end result is a very clean viz that will fit nicely in a well-designed dashboard.

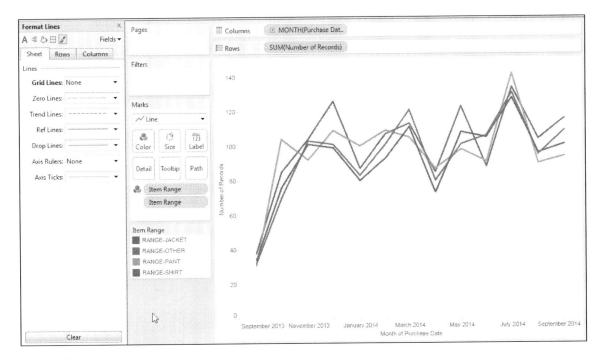

FIGURE 254: CLEAN VIZ

2. COPY / PASTE FORMATTING

Once you've taken the time to set up a chart or table exactly as you want it to be, you can use the formatting from that chart or table on other charts and tables in your workbook.

WORKED EXAMPLE: COPY AND PASTE FORMATTING

Simply go to "Format" on the toolbar and select "Copy Formatting".

FIGURE 255: "COPY FORMATTING"

Go to the chart or table you wish to apply that formatting to, go again to "Format" on the toolbar, but this time select "Paste Formatting".

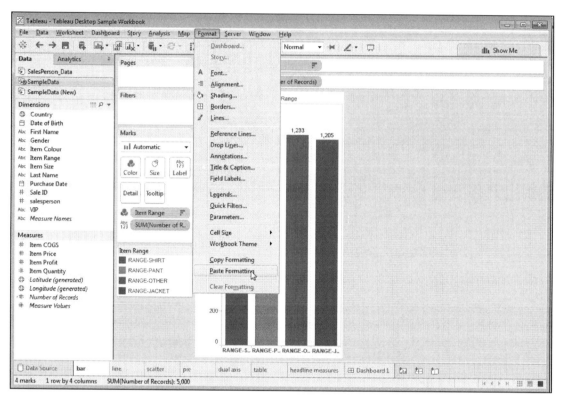

FIGURE 256: "PASTE FORMATTING"

The chart will update accordingly — in this example, notice how the outline and borders have been removed by applying these formatting fixes.

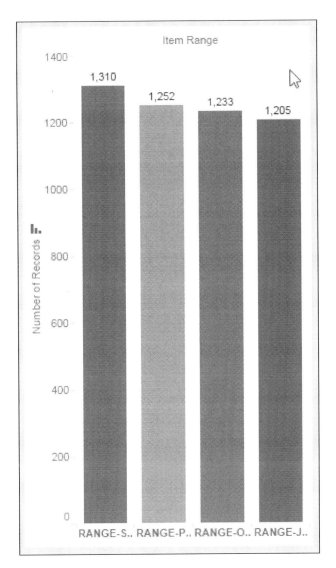

FIGURE 257: UPDATED BAR CHART

3. CUSTOM COLOUR PALETTES

I haven't come across a client yet that doesn't have a well-established — and often well policed! — corporate color palette. It only takes a few minutes to build a custom color palette that can be used in all your Tableau Desktop adventures.

First, we need to locate your Tableau Preferences File. Using WordPad or NotePad, go to the following location and open the file, preferences.ini\Documents\My Tableau Repository

If you can't find the file in this location, a quick search of your computer should locate the file.

WORKED EXAMPLE: CREATING CUSTOM COLOR PALETTES

Open the Tableau Preferences file in a text editor and look for the following text:

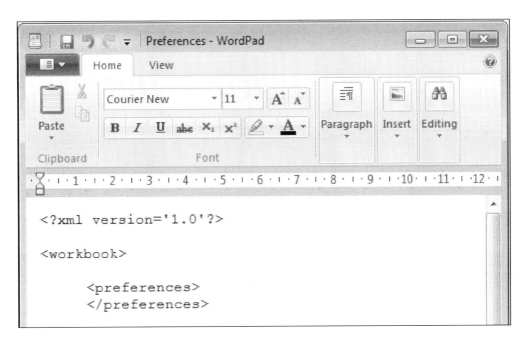

FIGURE 258: TABLEAU PREFERENCES FILE

Create some space between these two lines so you can add a new custom color palette that will load each time you open Tableau Desktop.

Between these two lines, simply copy the following text

```
<color-palette name="NAME" type="regular" >

     <color>#123456</color>
     <color>#123456</color>
     <color>#123456</color>
     <color>#123456</color>

</color-palette>
```

Replace "NAME" with a name for your palette (i.e. "Company Colors") and replace each of the #123456 values with the HEX value for each color. If your color palette needs more than four colors, simply copy and paste additional lines of <color>#123456</color>.

Save the preferences file and restart Tableau Desktop.

The next time you open Tableau Desktop, you will see your custom color palette is available when you edit the colors of your viz.

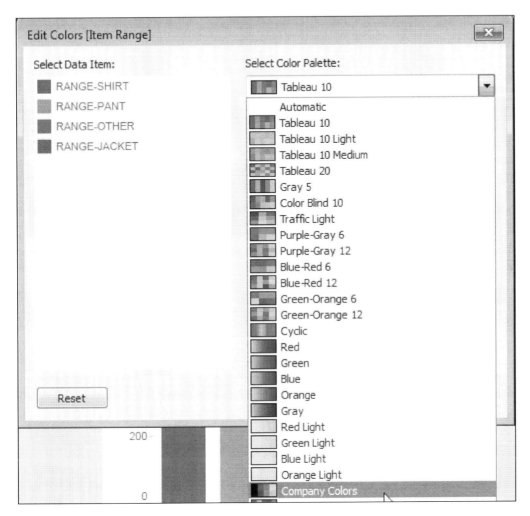

FIGURE 259: CUSTOM COLOR PALETTE

4. CUSTOM SHAPES

Creating a custom shape palette is a little easier. Simply locate your shapes files (which are likely to be at the following location: \Documents\My TableauRepository\Shapes) and create a new folder for your custom shapes.

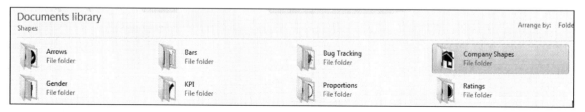

FIGURE 260: SHAPES FILES

WORKED EXAMPLE: CREATE CUSTOM SHAPE PALETTES

Copy and paste any images you wish to use as shapes in your visualizations into your new custom shape folder. I recommend keeping the shapes as simple as possible, and if you keep the shapes black in color so that you can also apply a color palette across the shapes as required.

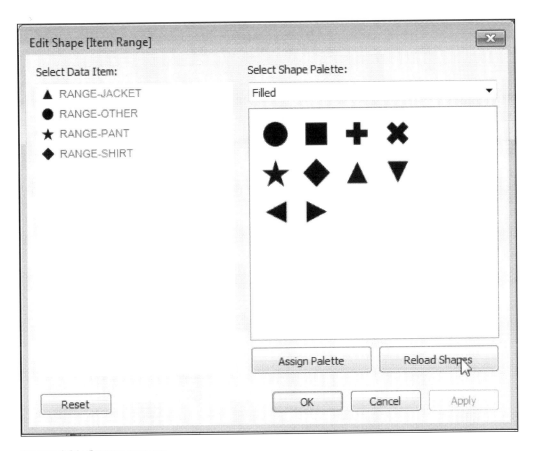

FIGURE 261: SHAPES IMAGES

Edit the shapes on your viz and click "Reload Shapes".

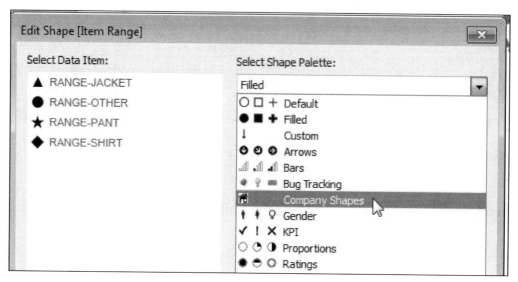

FIGURE 262: "RELOAD SHAPES"

Your custom shape palette will now be available for you to use in your viz!

WHERE TO FROM HERE?

The wider Tableau Community is phenomenally generous with their tips, advice and assistance. I always encourage my clients to take full advantage of the vast array of resources available to assist you — and help you expand your Tableau skill set.

Some of the key resources I recommend looking at, if not subscribing to, are:

- **Viz of the day**

    A daily email roundup of the best of the Tableau Public gallery. This is a handy way to stay up to date with the latest trends in data viz and see how other Tableau addicts have pushed the boundaries of Tableau Desktop to create awe-inspiring dashboards and visualizations.

    Another great feature is that because the featured vizes are hosted on Tableau Public, they are available to download so you can see how they were constructed.

    http://www.tableau.com/public/community/viz-of-the-day

- **Tableau Public**

If you're not so keen on receiving daily doses of Tableau goodness to your inbox, maybe try scheduling half an hour or so every other week to browse the Tableau Public galleries for yourself.

http://public.tableau.com

- **Data viz blogs**

There are countless data viz blogs – each with their own twist and each with their own data-rockstar at the helm. Try a google search to find the top ranking data viz blogs and see what style resonates with you. You could also search twitter for #tableau and #dataviz tweets to find some of the more active members of the Tableau community and check out their websites and blogs.

- **Tableau User Groups**

Tableau encourages people to share and explore together, to this end they support a range of local user groups worldwide. To find your nearest user group, visit the following link:

http://community.tableau.com/community/groups

If you can't find a local user group, why not start your own, or join one of the virtual user groups to connect with like-minded Tableau users.

- **Tableau Roadshows and the annual Conference**

If data-viz is your thing, you absolutely must get to either a local roadshow or the annual customer conference — or both! These events bring customers — just like you — to the stage to share their stories, their trials and their tribulations.

Aside from being an excellent opportunity to rub shoulders with those-in-the-Tableau-know, these events also incorporate a range of hands-on workshops where you can work with Tableau Pros to hone your craft. Details of upcoming roadshows and conferences are posted on the Tableau website:

http://www.tableau.com

- **Tableau Partners, Qualified Associates and Certified Professionals**

In addition to the growing user community who take pride in sharing their tips and advice with each other, there are also a number of Tableau Partners, Qualified Associates and Certified Professionals who produce a range of materials demonstrating new skills, tackling tricky issues and generally supporting the Tableau community.

Check out Performance Analytics at http://www.performanceanalytics.com.au to subscribe to our newsletter and receive our tips, tricks and hacks — as well as receive access to a wide range of support tools developed for business users, such as yourself!

- **Just jump in!**

Finally, the best way to learn Tableau is to learn by doing — practice makes perfect. Make mistakes, try again. Learn from other people. Have a look at Tableau Public and their "Viz of the Day". Have a look at what they have done. See if you can recreate that. It might give you inspiration for some ways that you could incorporate visualizations into other part of your business.

INDEX

Actions 218	Dashboards 24, 232	Fiscal Year 71
Add to Saved Data Sources....113	Data Source 19	Fit 239
Adding color 139	Data Visualization 132	Fit Height 239
Adding labels 141	Data viz blogs 284	Fit Image 241
Aliases 92	Default Date Formats 68	Fit Width 239
All on Dashboard 249	Default number format 52	Floating objects 256
Bar Chart 132	Default Settings 52	Formatting dashboards 238
Blending data 72	Default strings format 53	Geographic Maps 157
Calculated Fields 98	Dimensions 20	Geographic Role 167
Cards 21	Drag and Drop Data Connections 47	Headline measures 242
Clear Aliases 96	Dual Axis 195	Hide Title 240
Connect to Data 32	Dual Axis Charts 188	Interactivity 253
Copy Formatting 273	Duplicate as Crosstab 211	Latitude 159
Create Calculated Field 98	Edit Alias 93	Line charts 143
Creating a basic dashboard 234	Edit Axis 155	Live connections 117
Creating an Extract 123	Edit Data Source 115	Longitude 159
Creating Bar Charts 133	Edit Relationships 77	Marks card 21
Creating calculated fields 103	Edit shape 173	Measure Names 200
Creating dual axis charts 189	Edit Sizes 161	Measures 20
Creating geographic maps 158	Export Packaged Workbook ... 127	Metadata 121
Creating Line Charts 144	Extract Data 123	New Data Source 33
Creating pie charts 178	Extracts 117	Number of Records 54
Creating Scatter plots 170	Field Names 92	Paste Data 51
Crosstabs 211	Filter across multiple items 243	Paste formatting 272
Currency 61	Filtering Dates 225	Percent of total 213
Custom color palettes 276	Filtering Strings 219	Pie Charts 177
Custom date format 206	Filters 218	Pills 22
Custom Relationships 77	Filters card 21	Print to PDF 264
Custom shapes 280		Publish to Server 108

Publish Workbook 128	Sharing Data Sources 107	Tableau Server 259
Quick filters 247	Shelves 22	Tableau User Groups 284
Range of dates 227	Show Quick Filter 230	Tables 211
Refreshing Extracts 126	Starting and Ending dates 227	Tiled objects 256
Relative dates 226	Table calculations 213	Totals and subtotals 213
Removing grid lines 265	Tableau Community 283	Use as filter 253
Removing lines 265	Tableau Conference 285	Using extracts 121
Removing outlines 265	Tableau Online 260	Vary sizes by range 162
Replace Data Source 118	Tableau Preferences File 276	Viz and Vizes 23
Rotate Label 208	Tableau Public 261	Viz of the day 283
Running sum 214	Tableau Public gallery 283	Worksheets 23
Scatter Plots 169	Tableau Reader 263	
Scheduling and Authentication 130	Tableau Roadshows 285	

ABOUT THE AUTHOR

Jane Crofts, founder and Managing Director of Performance Analytics, draws on a wealth of experience in business analysis, management consulting, supply chain re-engineering and process improvement to lead a new era of executive information systems for the business community.

As one of the first Tableau Partners in Australia, a well-regarded Tableau specialist and Tableau Qualified Associate, Jane has worked with a range of clients through all aspects of their Tableau journey — from inception to development and production of striking and engaging dashboards and management information systems.

Made in the USA
Lexington, KY
27 April 2016